Nature's Way on Kiawah

A BARRIER ISLAND ON THE CAROLINA COAST

By

Bob Cowgill

With Illustrations by Janet Ellis

BOBCAT PRESS
KIAWAH ISLAND, SOUTH CAROLINA

Nature's Way on Kiawah

Front cover photograph of twin fawns and doe by Mark Permar
© 1995 Mark Permar
Back cover photograph of woodpeckers by Robert W. Cowgill
Author's photograph by Nancy Cowgill
© 1998 Robert W. Cowgill

Cover design by Aramais Andonian
Book design, typography & electronic pagination by Arrow Graphics, Inc.
Watertown, Massachusetts
Printed in the United States of America

**Library of Congress Catalog Card Number: 97-94679
ISBN: 0-9661595-0-0**

"As Thoreau found a universe in the woods around Concord, any person whose senses are alive can make a world of any natural place, however limited it might seem, on this subtle planet of ours."

Edward Abbey in *Down the River*

For Addie and Stan,
my mentor in computerland
Enjoy!
Bob Cowgill

Acknowledgments

Many of these stories could not have been written without the numerous volunteers from among the island residents who made possible the protective programs for wildlife on the island. Only a few of these wonderful, concerned individuals could be mentioned by name in these stories; however, all of them know of my deep gratitude.

Other stories could not have been written had it not been for the dedicated members of the South Carolina Department of Natural Resources. Sally and Tom Murphy, Charlotte Hope, Mark Dodd, John Cely, and Walt Rhodes have been especially protective of the wildlife on Kiawah, and I thank them all for allowing me to participate.

Among employees on the island, Major Baynard Seabrook of Security, Elizabeth King of the Recreation Department and Norm Shea as lake management supervisor have been deeply involved in the protection of wildlife on the island. They have skillfully mediated between the wildlife and the increasing pressure of humans.

I am grateful for the valuable suggestions by my wife, Nancy, and friends, Stephany Dunfee and Linda Malcolm, regarding the content of the Introductory section of the manuscript. The cover photograph by Kiawah photographer Mark Permar expresses *Nature's Way on Kiawah* in a beautiful, graphic fashion. The expertise of Dale Anderson was essential in the design of the map of Kiawah on his computer. All of their advice and help should aid the reader, unfamiliar with Kiawah Island, to find his or her way about in these stories.

Finally, recognition should be given to that mythological cougar that haunts our sense of the mystery and wildness that still lingers on Kiawah.

Table of Contents

Preface

Kiawah Island, just south of Charleston, South Carolina, is one of the barrier islands that form a bulwark against the sea along the southern portion of the state. Ten miles of gently sloping beach face the Atlantic Ocean, and a vast saltmarsh segmented by the Kiawah River separates the island from the mainland. Exciting events occur on the beach and in the marsh at all seasons of the year. Also, there are the lively doings, sometimes amusing and sometimes tragic, of the numerous animals and birds that visit and in many cases live year-round in the ponds and forests of live oak, pine and palmetto. All have constituted grist for the mill that is *Nature's Way on Kiawah*.

The stories in this collection first appeared in *Kiawah Island Talk*, a newspaper published by the Kiawah Properties Owners Group, Inc. for distribution to its members. The stories were written for a monthly column to inform members about events on Kiawah Island that relate to its natural beauty and the wildlife that share the island with us. Stories for the period 1992–1995 were published in 1996 in a book entitled *Nature Trails*.

It is my hope that the present collection of more recent stories will renew cherished memories for faithful readers of the column, and bring to new readers an awareness of the drama of living on a tiny barrier island.

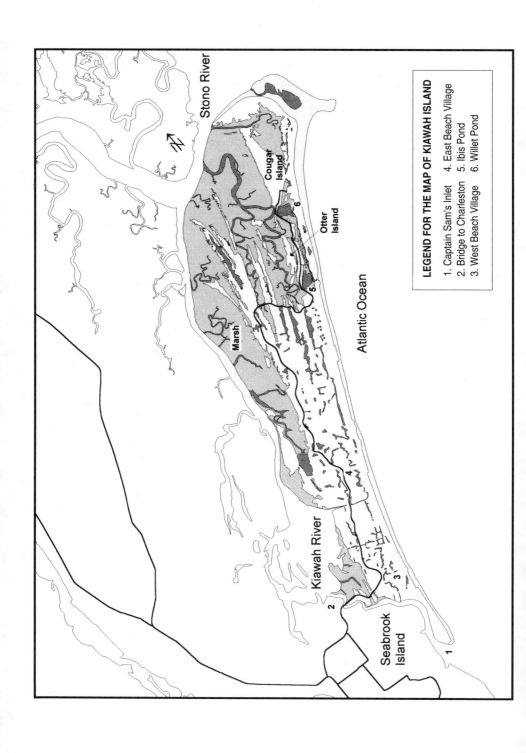

LEGEND FOR THE MAP OF KIAWAH ISLAND

1. Captain Sam's Inlet   4. East Beach Village
2. Bridge to Charleston   5. Ibis Pond
3. West Beach Village   6. Willet Pond

Stono River

Atlantic Ocean

Kiawah River

Marsh

Cougar Island

Otter Island

Seabrook Island

An Introduction to Kiawah Island

Nature's Way of Forming a Barrier Island

J ust to be on a barrier island creates a feeling of excitement in most of us. The name suggests that the island must serve as a protective barrier for the mainland. Because a barrier island arises from changes in sea level and the movement of sand by ocean currents, it is subject to continual modification both in size and shape. Realization of the transitory nature of the island adds to the sense of excitement, and a desire to know more about its origin.

The barrier islands along the Carolina-Georgia coast were formed at the end of the last glacial epoch about 15,000 years ago. At that time incredible amounts of water were retained in vast glaciers, and the sea level was about 150 feet lower than today. Therefore, the South Carolina coast was many miles out on what is now the continental shelf. When global climates changed, the glaciers began to melt and the sea level rose. It is thought that the invading water inundated the coastal valleys and created a jagged shoreline. Waves immediately began to reshape the coast by cutting away the headlands that protruded into the sea. As the sea level continued to rise the remnants of these headlands became detached from the mainland, and the barrier islands were born.

These barrier islands did not disappear beneath the waves as the sea level continued to rise; instead, they migrated toward the mainland. This natural migratory process continues today, and is called beach erosion by owners of oceanfront property. Needless to say more and more of the mainland also was submerged by the rising sea level and so the coastline also retreated, leaving the barrier islands still separated from the mainland by rivers, estuaries and vast marshes.

Dr. Miles Hayes of the University of South Carolina studied this process in the 1970s. He found that the effects of a combination of tidal range, longshore currents and inlet locations determined the shape of each barrier island. They all seemed to acquire characteristic shapes that he termed the "hot dog" and the "drum stick."

As the map of Kiawah Island shows, it clearly has the "drum stick" shape. The eastern portion is thickened by sand deposition from the outflow of the Stono River as well as sand carried down from Folly Beach to the northeast. By contrast, the western portion of the island is the narrow end of the "drum stick;" it is shaped by the whittling away of sand by the Kiawah River on the landward side and by the longshore current on the ocean side.

It may surprise you to note that the island has an east-west orientation, but if you stand anywhere on the ten miles of beach, do not look out over the ocean for your sunrises—they will be off to your left at the thick portion of the "drumstick." You may also observe that the meandering Kiawah River and a huge marsh separate Kiawah Island from neighboring islands and the mainland. In between the marsh and the beach, the central portion of the island contains approximately 4000 acres of land elevated five feet or more above mean sea level. At one time, this was largely a maritime forest dominated by live oaks, pines and palmettos. Today, this forest is in the process of being replaced by the homes, roads and golf courses of a modern civilization.

A Brief History
of Kiawah Island

As just related, a barrier island is continually changing. That pattern of change runs all through the history of Kiawah Island. The age of clam shells at various depths in the foundations of Kiawah, as determined by radioactive techniques, indicate that the present island was formed about 4000 years ago. In that period of rising sea level, sand accumulated around the roots of a more ancient landmass that probably was the rocky ridge that first formed the barrier island. Those roots are located beneath what we call Rhetts Bluff and along a portion of the Kiawah Island Parkway.

Even now, the island is imperceptibly migrating in response to the rising sea level. Peat beds protrude through the beach sand at the eastern end of Kiawah, and they graphically confirm this migration. These peat beds formed long ago in the marsh behind the island and it is possible to find embedded in them the shells of oysters and species of clams that grow only in the marsh. Since the time the shells were embedded, the island has migrated shoreward until those ancient beds now reappear on the seaward side of the island.

Once the sandbar that was destined to become Kiawah Island had grown to a size sufficient to have some stability, vegetation appeared. Kiawah probably then resembled other undisturbed barrier islands that still exist, clothed in brush and a mixture of palmettos, pines and hardwoods. But Kiawah did not remain undisturbed. The island responded to storms and ocean currents that continually altered the size and shape of its perimeter. In the interior, the vegetation was destroyed many times by hurricanes and by fires arising from lightning or set by Indians.

The Indians had visited the island long before recorded history to hunt game and gather shellfish. A small tribe called the Kiawahs used the island for that purpose at the time the first white settlers arrived. They and the Ashepoos, Edistos, Sewees and Wandos all lived in tiny coastal villages of small, round huts of palmetto thatch. Each tribe was separated from the others by natural barriers, the rivers that now bear their tribal names. A lack of fresh water and soil too poor for even their meager crops of corn, peas and beans precluded the establishment of permanent camps on the barrier islands. Today the only traces of these indigenous people that called this coast home are the shell middens such as the one to be seen on Rhett's Bluff that dates back to approximately 1500 BC.

When the Europeans arrived profound changes occurred. Much of the history of that time has been summarized in *The History and Archaeology of Kiawah Island, Charleston County, South Carolina* (Chicora Foundation Research Series 30). By 1675 the naïve Kiawah Indians had been persuaded to cede their lands, including Kiawah Island, to the English for "cloth, hatchets, brads & other manufacturers," and by the 1740s they had disappeared from the pages of history. The Lords Proprietors, who controlled the land, granted Kiawah Island to Captain George Raynor in 1699. Captain Raynor may have procured his investment capital in the piracy business, and he was only the first of many colorful characters to acquire possession of Kiawah land.

Indications are that early in the 18th Century it was used as a cattle range; the animals were conveniently confined to the island and there was a plentiful supply of salt hay (*Spartina patens*) along the marsh that provided excellent fodder. The island underwent a large change when the plantation owners, the Shoolbreds, Stanyarnes and Vanderhorsts, realized that profits were to be made by growing indigo and cotton. A map dated 1854 shows that contiguous agricultural fields occupied the entire middle third of the island, and the 1860 Agricultural Census listed 800 acres of improved and 1700 acres of unimproved land in the Vanderhorst plantation.

Following the Civil War and the general stagnation of the southern economy, the fields were abandoned and nature began to recloth the island in brush and trees. By the time of the purchase of the island by C.C. Royal in 1950, that transition was well along. Under the ownership of Mr. Royal, a different set of changes began. He viewed the island from a lumberman's perspective and extensively removed marketable pine. One exception was at the eastern end where Coastguardsmen stationed on the island at the time of the First World War had put so many steel-jacketed bullets in the trees during target practice that saw blades were destroyed at his mills.

Several of the old logging roads became the forerunners of our Kiawah Island Parkway, Governor's Drive and Ocean Course Drive. It was at this time that most of the large ponds on the island also were created by diking off fingers of the marsh in the construction of logging roads.

A different cast of owners took center stage when the Kiawah Island Company purchased the island in 1974. That real-estate development company set in motion a different series of changes that continue to this day. A decision on the merits of these changes will vary with the viewer, but changes will continue for that is the very essence of barrier islands.

Nature's Way of Stabilizing the Beach

Our beach is responsive to both wind and wave. Storm waves of winter erode the beach, and the sand is redistributed to form a wide, flat beach. The beach fights back in this way, because the gentle slope diminishes the force of incoming waves and protects the upper beach from extensive damage. Even though some winter storms cut steep banks, these heal as the sand dries and the banks collapse under the influence of wind and wave. The shallow, long waves of summer restore the dunes by acting in concert with the wind to pile up sand at the upper beach.

Mats of brown reeds from the marsh wash ashore in the spring and stabilize the beach. It is true that the mats are rather unsightly when they are present, and they do impede the progress of all—from sunbathers to nesting marine turtles. However, this inconvenience is adequately compensated by the large amount of sand retained on the beach by their presence. This is done in two ways. The first and most obvious way is that the mats accumulate blown sand and begin the build-up of dunes. The second benefit is less obvious, but if one looks closely at the mats, tiny sprigs of new green vegetation may be seen. The mats are serving as a mulch and nursery for new plants that also stabilize the beach, both by diminishing the force of wind and by retaining the sand at high tides.

This is part of a grand cycle that occurs annually. In the marsh, spartina grass sprouts early in the spring from the roots of the previous growth and rises to heights of 4 to 6 feet. In winter, the grass dies, and the dried reeds are washed out of the marsh by high tides the following spring. The reeds are carried to the sea by the Kiawah and Stono Rivers, transferred further by the ocean currents and deposited along our beach. Thus, the physical forces of wind and wave work in concert with plant-life to stabilize our island of sand.

However, other changes may have a more profound effect on the size and shape of the beach. The most dramatic change within historical times occurred when the jetties were constructed at the entrance to Charleston Harbor in the period 1878–96. One consequence was the change of the longshore currents, which led to extensive erosion of the beaches of Folly and Morris Islands. The eroded sand moved southwest due to prevailing ocean currents and much of it was deposited at the eastern end of Kiawah. By the early 1940s the eastern end of the island had advanced 3,400 feet as determined by Professor Miles Hayes and his students at the USC Geology department during their studies of the Kiawah beach.

The shoreline at the eastern end of the island still fluctuates in response to the periodic accumulation of sand shoals in the ebb tidal delta of the Stono Inlet. When a shoal builds up, the longshore current that normally runs from east to west and parallel to the beach may be deflected landward, and erosion may occur at the center of the beach. After the shoal migrates and attaches along the easternmost mile of Kiawah's shoreline, sand is distributed all along the beach, and the erosion usually is reversed. The overall impact of shoal attachment has been positive for Kiawah, and just in the past half century over 12 million cu.yds. have been gained along the Kiawah beach. Another way of viewing this is that the shoals are an immense reservoir of sand for natural renourishment of the beach after storms.

Ocean currents and storms often cut inlets through the central portion of long barrier islands such as Kiawah, and two existed here for a very long time—indeed they are shown on the first known chart of the island, dated 1661. These two inlets were located at what are now Ibis and Willet ponds. When the inlets existed, tidal flow occurred between the ocean and creeks on the Kiawah River side of the island. Therefore, Otter and Cougar were truly islands and separate from the main island we call Kiawah. (Refer to the map on page viii.) Creation of a dike for a road to haul timber resulted in closure of the inlet at Ibis pond in the 1950s; and a similar dike at what was to become Willet pond caused the second inlet to close sometime between aerial photographs made in 1963 and in 1973.

We can be thankful for these changes, because we now have one of the best of the barrier island beaches in the state. *The Annual State of the Beaches Report* of the S.C. Coastal Council for 1993 tersely stated, "Kiawah is one of the most stable islands in the state, although the eastern and western ends of the island are more dynamic due to their proximity to inlets. Development on Kiawah is set well landward of the primary dune line." Thank you for those kind words. Lets do what we can to keep the beach that way for all to enjoy for a very long time.

One important way to preserve the beach is to protect the dunes. The vegetation that grows there stabilizes the dunes quite well, but much of it, although it appears tough, is living precariously and easily destroyed by a careless footstep. Therefore, all entry to the beach should be via the regular walkways that afford excellent views of the dunes and its vegetation. For the same reason, sunbathers should respect the vegetation when they place their chairs and blankets.

The Marsh: Nature's Nursery For the Sea

The marsh is one of the great resources of Kiawah Island, and the equal of the beach in importance. Offshore sandbars, the beach and dunes, they all stabilize the island by buffering against ocean currents and storms. In similar fashion, the wide saltwater marsh with its green carpet of tall grass protects the island by buffering against erosion by river currents and the powerful surge-waves that accompany storms such as Hurricane Hugo in 1989.

The marsh grass stands virtually as a monoculture of *Spartina alternaflora*, commonly referred to as spartina or cordgrass. In the absence of the grass with its dense network of roots, the river would erode the banks of soft mud and meander back and forth from Kiawah Island to Johns Island on the other side. So that at one time the river might be far away and then again be under the doorsteps of homes on the marsh side of the island. There is a continual contest between the tight root mass for retention of the soil and the river for sweeping it away. The plant roots are joined in this contest by the cooperative action of the ribbed mussels that fasten their shells to the roots by strong fibers called byssus. Thus, the molluscs form a bulwark reminiscent of the riprap that man uses to stabilize banks.

The marsh has another important role; it serves as the nursery for huge numbers of marine organisms by providing food and shelter. Decaying marsh grass contributes the vast bulk of the detritus that is the basic food, but other important contributions come from the algae that grow on the mud and the plankton brought in from the sea by each tide. Added to this huge food supply is the large amount of animal and plant life brought into the marsh on each tide. This material comes both from the freshwater streams inland and the salt water of the sea.

The salinity of the river varies greatly from day to day, as these two sources of fresh- and salt-water mix; heavy rains raise the amount of fresh water, storms at sea push more seawater into the river and render it more saline. Most of the animals and plants brought into the marsh by the tidal flow cannot adjust to these large excursions in salinity and perish, thus adding their bodies to the food supply. The juvenile stages of most crabs, fish and shrimp also are carried into the marsh by the tidal flow, however, these organisms can withstand the fluctuations in salinity. The larger fishes that would consume these juveniles dare not penetrate the dense stand of spartina, and those that do often become entrapped and perish when the water recedes. Thus, abundant food and shelter make the marsh an ideal nursery; and when the juveniles mature and leave the marsh for the open sea, their multitudes renew the ocean for another year.

The tidal creeks offer a different habitat. Here, the large predatory fish such as red drum, spotted sea-trout and flounder enter with the inflow of tidal water, but they must be careful to retreat in time to avoid the muddy waters of the rivulets at low tide when temperatures soar and dissolved oxygen levels plunge. Two interesting mammals time their visits to these creeks at the high tide. One is the Bottlenose dolphin that comes into the creeks from the Kiawah River. These seemingly happy-go-lucky characters pursue the fish and herd them up on the mud banks for easy capture. Other marsh residents take advantage of the sudden bonanza, and even the timid Sora rail may dash from the cover of the grass beds to snatch up a tidbit. Occasionally, a dolphin will misjudge the tide and become stranded. But usually, these somehow manage to survive until the next tide lifts them free.

The other mammal is truly a marsh animal, it is the River otter. It too enters the creeks at high tide, for it does not seem to enjoy trudging about over the oyster shells and bottom muck. However, when the tide comes in, it leaves the inland pond, bounds along over the dike and into the creek. You will know it is around, because it is a creature of habit and forms a well-worn path on each side of the dike bank.

Denizens of the mud flats also must adjust their lives to the tidal rhythm. For example, the fiddler crabs actively search for food and mates at low tide, but as the water rises, they dash down, each to its own burrow, plug the entrance with mud and wait out the high tide. Periwinkle snails, that have been grazing on the algae, climb stalks of spartina to avoid the water and the predators that come in with the rising water. Those that enter with the tide include the mud crabs and blue crabs to scavenge the organisms that did not escape the rising water.

Most of the birds that visit the marsh adjust their arrival to match the tide and their method of feeding. Laughing gulls in search of fiddler crabs wait for the low tide to soar above the bands of crabs as they roam over the exposed mud flats. The egrets and herons too await the low tide to patrol the creek beds, for then the fish and crabs are concentrated in shallow pools and are easy prey. By contrast, the migratory ducks in winter prefer the creeks at high tide; they depart for the river, ocean or inland ponds as the water recedes.

Other rhythms, also determined by solar events, proceed more slowly. I refer to the seasonal changes as planet earth slowly wobbles in its orbit around the sun. Like the endless cycle of the tides, creatures of the marsh ebb and flow with the seasons. With the shorter days of fall, creek fauna decline both in numbers and variety. The immense carpet of marsh grass also responds. In fall, it turns a lovely amber shade and then as winter advances, the stalks darken and die to add to the mulch that will be needed in the coming spring. But even as the plants die back, sprouts of new growth rise from the perennial roots to create the marsh of the coming year.

Beyond all these features, the visual impact of that vast expanse is its most rewarding attribute for most of us. From one of the viewing towers, the Kiawah River is defined in the distance by a slender shimmer of open water and the occasional boat with its sails skimming over the marsh like the white wings of the egret. Closer by, the islets in the marsh resemble ships in a sea of grass; all sailing the same east-west course for they are the remnants of the same ancient dunes that make up Kiawah itself. The view is rendered even more dramatic by the approach of a storm coming off Johns Island—so small and insignificant in the distance, so powerful when it suddenly sweeps over the marsh and hits with its full fury. In sunnier times, it is peaceful to watch the slow progress of cloud shadows, and the wind patterns as the marsh grass bends in response. Add the majestic sweeping strokes of the Blue heron, the meandering course of a small family of raccoons heading out at low tide or the Lilliputian battles and courtships of the fiddler crabs at our feet, and the scene is complete.

Some of the Interesting Wildlife That You May Encounter

Alligators
That Bask Beside
the Ponds

You may see alligators swimming in the water or basking on the bank of almost any small lagoon or larger pond on the island during the warmer months of the year. These prehistoric beasts are striving to live out their days just as their ancestors have done for millions of years, but this becomes increasingly difficult as the human population increases. The gators are happy to leave the humans alone, if only the humans would do the same for them. If molested, they may hiss in protest, especially at the time for mating in the spring and during the summer nesting season. Seldom will they be more aggressive unless they have lost their natural fear of humans, usually because they have been fed. However, they are not restrained as are those in a zoo; children should be warned never to approach them, and pets should not be allowed to roam freely. Perhaps if visitors to the island learn more about this fascinating animal, they will respect its right to exist on the island and admire it from a safe distance.

The American alligator (*Alligator mississippiensis*) has been cruising the waterways of the south beneath trees festooned with Spanish moss for untold thousands of years. Early explorers staggered out of the swamps with terrifying tales of the size and ferocity of these beasts. However, settlers soon realized their value both for food and leather, and for many years they were either treated as vermin or exploited for their economic value. Young alligators were killed, stuffed and sold as curios to the tourists from up north, while shoes and handbags were man- ufactured in large quantities from the hides of adults.

In this century, South Carolinians became concerned about the decreasing number of alligators in the state. By 1962, only licensed trappers could capture alligators; then, the alligator season was completely closed after 1964, and alligator popula- tions started an impressive comeback. Today, there are about six hundred alligators in the ponds on Kiawah Island, and these range in size from 8 inch hatchlings to one male that measured 12 $1/2$ feet from snout to tail tip and weighed over 500 pounds! Not many approach that size; most adult males are about 9 feet long, and the smaller females average 7 $1/2$ feet as adults.

In spring, the thoughts of alligators turn to the opposite sex, and they will roam far and wide in search of a mate. In the process, the alligator may inadvertently end up in someone's garage or swimming pool to the consternation of all concerned. Courtship is long and elaborate, and bellowing is an important component. Bellowing usually occurs in the early morning, and it serves to attract both sexes to a pond where there might be a potential mate. Only males were thought to bellow, but now it is known that females bellow a different tune to attract courting males. She may be quite successful at this and attract a number of males. Usually the largest male will aggressively drive the other males from the pond before approaching the female.

Courtship begins in a leisurely fashion as the male and female touch snouts, rub heads and emit coughing sounds. The male can be surprisingly gentle with the female at this time. The pair may circle one another, press close together, part, intertwine, submerge and blow bubbles. This may go on for quite some time, with pauses while they float quietly as though studying each other. Sometime during this process, mating occurs—often beneath the water.

By mid-summer, the female will find a nesting site for her eggs. The site is frequently a secluded location near a lagoon bank. The alligator constructs the nest from pond vegetation and mud that she carries in her mouth and shapes with her body and tail to form a mound about five feet across and two feet high. It is well camouflaged and from a safe distance, it may look like a pile of dead reeds and grasses. She makes a depression in the top of the mound and deposits about 40 leathery, white eggs that resemble goose eggs. Those who have watched the egg-laying procedure state that as each egg leaves her body, the female meets it with the underside of her hind limb, first breaking the fall and then positioning the egg in the nest. After the last egg has been deposited, she covers the clutch; with amazing control, she grasps vegetation with the claws of her hind limb and lays it over the eggs. And there they will incubate over the next two months as the mother stands guard nearby to challenge all intruders, including raccoons and humans.

Upon hatching, the tiny alligators are quite attractive with their jet-black skin set off with conspicuous yellow cross-bands. The mother uncovers the nest, aids the hatchlings to the water and may even carry some of them there in her jaws. Once in the water, the hatchlings will stay close together near the nest site. They often crawl upon the mother's head and back where they bask in the sun and snap at passing insects. In spite of this good maternal care, young alligators are preyed upon heavily by raccoons, otters, turtles, and the herons and egrets. Only the few that attain adult size will be safe from predators other than man. Let's leave them in peace to spend their lives on the banks and in the ponds of Kiawah.

White-tailed Deer That Roam the Woods

White-tailed deer are native to barrier islands such as Kiawah, and they thrive in our community today, despite vigorous hunting in the past and the current loss of habitat. It has been estimated that there are about six or seven hundred deer on the island, and they are a delight to see as they move alertly and gracefully through the forest. They are as much a part of the natural landscape as the beautiful birds and smaller animals.

But sharing the island with us creates a number of problems. Deer are most active from dusk to dawn as they wander about and browse a variety of vegetation. When attempting to cross a road, they may be struck by a passing car. The result often is death for the deer, extensive damage to the vehicle and sometimes serious injury to the occupants. Therefore, a caution to motorists is in order: slow down and be especially alert while driving at night! Another problem arises from the fecundity of female deer. Depending on age, health and environmental factors, a doe will give birth to one, two, or sometimes three fawns each year. Consequently, their numbers can increase rapidly, consumption of expensive plants for landscaping can be serious, and of course, the frequency of vehicle accidents will increase.

Fawns normally are born in May and June. Well developed and weighing five or six pounds, fawns try to stand almost immediately. The doe thoroughly checks her newborn, washes it with her tongue and sometimes is so vigorous that she sends it sprawling. Because the fawn is so unsteady on its feet, the mother may even lie down to give it the first drink of rich milk, fortified with almost three times the fat and protein of cow's milk. About an hour after birth, a fawn will be able to walk, and the mother will lead it to a more protected spot and leave it there. It will remain alone, as if asleep, silently curled up in the cover the mother has selected. Its tawny-red coat, speckled with numerous white spots, is excellent camouflage, and it is without any odor that might attract a predator.

The doe will return every few hours to clean and nurse the fawn. She also keeps an eye out for predators and will arrive, sharp hooves flying, if she senses danger to her baby. People who assume that a lone fawn is abandoned, particularly if it is bleating, are usually wrong. The person should not even approach the fawn, because the doe can detect the odor of a human on her baby, and she may temporarily or even permanently desert it. When about 2 weeks old, a fawn begins to follow its mother. Although it will nurse often and will not be weaned for three months, the fawn starts sampling grasses and twigs in just a few weeks.

For the rest of the year, family groups of mothers and female fawns usually stay together, but the young males are excluded as they develop into bucks. Buck deer change from shy creatures of the forest to aggressive males whose behavior is often unpredictable. The reason is hormonal changes in the animals at the season of "rut." This is the climax of a series of changes; most of them triggered by alterations in hormonal levels that occur in both male and female deer as they prepare for the annual mating season. In early spring the bucks begin to form a new set of antlers to replace the ones cast off during the winter. These bony structures are initially sheathed in a soft skin called velvet and grow quite rapidly (sometimes as much as one or two inches in a week). As day length shortens in August and September, hormonal levels of testosterone increase and the antlers begin to harden. The mineralization of the antlers stimulates the bucks to vigorously rub their antlers on bushes or small trees to remove the velvet, much to the dismay of the home-owner who views the broken branches on his favorite shrub.

At this stage, the antlers have been converted into formidable weapons for the buck in its contests with other bucks for possession of a territory, and the opportunities to mate with the females as they come into estrus. You may see evidence of these contests as scuffed-up marks in your yard or even hear the rattling of the antlers as the bucks joust in the night. Sometimes this bellicose mood is so powerful that the buck challenges other animals and even humans. If you encounter a large buck standing erect, staring at you and perhaps even pawing the ground with his fore-hooves, don't accept the challenge. A retreat is the prudent course. In any event do not advance toward him with the idea of calling his bluff; an unarmed man is certain to lose that contest.

When all the fighting and breeding is over, bucks shed their antlers and settle down to a more sociable and quieter life. They band together with does and fawns to face the winter together. But then, the lengthening days of spring will drive them to repeat the entire cycle once again.

Loggerhead Turtles That Nest on the Beach

Five species of marine turtles, the Green, Hawksbill, Kemp's ridley, Leatherback and Loggerhead, pass by our shore, but only the Loggerhead nests here. You may never see it come ashore because that normally occurs at night, but the biologists can give a good description. The Loggerhead (*Caretta, caretta*, to give it the definitive scientific name) is quite variable in size from possibly 30 to 47 inches of carapace (top shell) length and weighs about 300 lb. for the adult female and 400 lb. or more for the male. It has a massive, blunt head from which it derives its name, for sailors upon seeing the raised head in the water often mistook it for a log. The outermost layer of plates on the shell and head are called scutes, and the number and position of the scutes are used to distinguish the various species. The Loggerhead is the most abundant of the five species in the western Atlantic, and it wanders widely in tropical and sub-tropical waters where it feeds on jellyfish, sponges and algae.

Loggerheads are of an ancient lineage, because their ancestors go back more than 150 million years. Today, their ancient lifestyle is threatened by human activities all over the world. The genetic traits and behavioral patterns that they developed over those vast periods made their survival possible. However, those traits are not flexible enough to permit them to adapt to the swift and drastic changes inflected upon their habitat by the recent arrival of man. Therefore, many of us feel impelled to do what we can to insure that they continue to survive and share with us this beautiful world they have known so very long.

I believe that property owners of Little Cumberland Island, Georgia began the first protection of a Loggerhead turtle rookery in 1964. Shortly thereafter, other people began to protect their rookeries, and the Kiawah Island program in 1972 was one of the early ones. Now, volunteers from among the Kiawah residents begin to patrol the beach in early May of each year.

The daily patrol starts at dawn and covers the entire ten miles of beach in a small all-terrain vehicle. When the crawl marks of a nesting turtle are encountered, the patrol members follow the tracks to the nesting site. They probe the sand carefully with a wooden dowel to locate the nest, and often they must relocate the eggs to a safer spot on the beach.

About 50 days later, patrol members will begin to observe the nest for signs of hatching. The emerging hatchlings leave an opening in the sand above the nest cavity and their tiny tracks leading toward the ocean permit an estimate to be made of their number. Three days later, the nest may be dug to liberate any stragglers and to evaluate the success of the nest. All of these activities are regulated by the SC Dept. of Natural Resources, and an annual report of the nesting patrol activities is required by that agency.

All of this protective activity by we humans is commendable and interesting, but the paramount story of the nesting comes from the activities of the turtles themselves. When the water warms on the continental shelf in spring, male and female turtles assemble to mate. After the mating period, the male departs but the female remains offshore while her fertilized eggs develop. Sometime in May, she lumbers ashore at night and begins the laborious struggle up the beach to a nesting site. She is wary at this time and easily frightened off by a noise or a carelessly shown flashlight; that is one reason for the motto, "Lights out for turtles."

Once she has selected a site, she slowly digs her nest with her back flippers, alternating one and then the other to withdraw a scoop of sand until she reaches the maximum depth, about 18 inches beneath the surface. She begins to deposit her eggs one at a time, and these fall to the bottom of the nest and pack together. Once the process has begun, she will continue even if disturbed by enthusiastic people shining lights in her eyes or equally enthusiastic raccoons stealing eggs at the rear. When the last of the 100–150 eggs have been deposited, she tops off the nest with sand, packs it down firmly by thumping her shell over it and throws sand all around the area with her flippers for concealment. Down the beach and into the waves she goes, never to return to the nest. She has done her part; now it is up to the next generation.

However, she doesn't do this just once in a season. After about 2 weeks, another clutch of eggs will develop from the original mating, and once again, and probably for a third and fourth time, she will trudge ashore to make other nests. Where is she during those periods between nestings? Information is fragmentary but the few radio-tagged females seem to wander about in local waters, and scuba divers often find turtles asleep beneath ledges close inshore. Finally, her nesting duties complete, she departs for the ocean, and she may skip a year or two before repeating the performance.

What happens in the nest she has left behind? If she has chosen a safe site, the eggs begin to develop. Each egg is remarkably like a Ping-Pong ball in appearance. It is round, white and covered with a parchment-like, pliable shell. The dark, moist nest cavity beneath the sand maintains a constant temperature day and night; therefore, it is a nearly ideal incubation chamber. The embryo develops over a period of about 55–60 days into a tiny turtle, all curled up within the shell. It grows a sharp spine on the tip of its snout called an egg tooth, and with that tooth it ruptures the shell and is able to leave the egg. Resting, sometimes for days within the nest cavity, it straightens its body and continues to consume the remnant of the attached yolk sac.

Then, restless stirring within the compact mass of little turtles activates them all, and they cooperatively struggle up through the sand to within perhaps a few inches of the surface. There they pause and wait again. What are they waiting for? They wait for the best time to leave the nest and make a dash for the ocean; that time is after nightfall when few predators are around, or least likely to see them. They seem to sense that time by the drop in temperature of the surface sand as the sun drops below the horizon. Then out they come in a rush and head for the water. How do they know which way to go? They head for the brightest mass they can see. In ancient times that was the wave-tops catching the light from the moon and stars. Now unfortunately, they may head toward a brightly lit home or streetlight with tragic results. Again, a reason for the motto, "Lights out for turtles."

Their scurrying trip down the beach to the water seems to set their guidance system; if they are carried down by misguided folks who want to save them the trip, the poor things circle round and round in the water as though bewildered. Once they reach the water on their own, they instantly change from a crawling gait to a swimming stroke and off they go as rapidly as possible. Here too the predators wait, because they are a welcome morsel for fish and crabs beneath the surface, and for gulls and other birds above.

For a long time, it was a mystery where they went. Now we are beginning to understand that they swim away from land in a frenzy until they encounter masses of sargassum and other seaweeds in the Gulf Stream possibly 20–30 kilometers offshore. Here in the shelter of the weeds, they remain and grow for an indeterminate length of time; then, they voyage out on their own into the vast ocean, navigating possibly by magnetic signals and wave direction. After a period of 20–25 years, the few survivors (perhaps one in ten thousand!) will gather off our coast to mate and nest. Hopefully they will receive a friendly and protective reception at that time from our children and grandchildren.

26

Migratory Ducks
That Visit In
the Winter

Visitors to Kiawah Island in the winter should be aware of the waterfowl that also visit our ponds and offshore waters at that season. Aside from the pleasure of seeing these beautiful birds, both in flight and on the water, they tell us something important about the state of health of our environment. Unlike the caged canaries that were carried beneath ground to warn miners of carbon monoxide gas in the mine shafts, the waterfowl are free to travel where they wish. Their presence assures us that the pond environment is healthy. It is possible to turn this around and consider the maintenance of the ponds in good condition as a means of preserving our duck species. It is important to protect the summer nesting ponds in the north as has been well publicized, but it is equally important to provide the migratory ducks a safe haven for their sojourn in the south in the winter. And this is just what Kiawah seems to be doing.

Often in winter immense flocks numbering in the thousands may be seen from the beach either floating on the surface of the sea in dark clusters called rafts, or flying in long black skeins silhouetted against the pearly white clouds of winter. Each duck will appear as a black dot on the water, far out from shore, but with the aid of a spotting scope they often may be identified as Scaup, small dark ducks with white side-panels. How they acquired such an unattractive name is not known. Possibly it is a rendition of the bird's call; if the poor bird had a more melodious voice, it might have been called a bobolink. Other species that we might expect to see there occasionally are Black scoters and Surf scoters, and on the periphery of some flocks may be a few members of other species such as Red-throated loons and Red-breasted mergansers.

If we now turn to the ponds in the interior of the island, we find that they range from many small ones of a fraction of an acre in size to large ponds such as Bass (33 acres) and Willet (40 acres). The ponds vary in depth, vegetation, salinity and other characteristics that make them more or less attractive for migratory ducks. The newer and generally smaller lagoons were created during the development of golf courses and real estate, and many of them do not have the protective vegetation and food resources to attract ducks. The older ponds, as mentioned earlier, were created about thirty or forty years ago by diking off fingers of marsh that lay between the ancient dunes that formed the island. Mr. Thomas C. Welch, Jr., the island caretaker from 1958 to 1973, has told me that the ponds were stocked with fish but were not intended to draw waterfowl for hunting. Over the years, however, vegetation has grown in these older ponds and now serves as good protective cover and food for a variety of both surface-feeding and diving species.

In recent winters, the Hooded mergansers have been present in largest numbers on many of the ponds. I will refer to as them as "Hoodies," an affectionate nickname given to them locally. So, when you see ducks on a pond, look at the heads, for the male Hoodies are easy to spot by a prominent white patch on the side of the head—the females are more modestly cloaked in brown. These engaging little diving ducks have a slender bill with serrate structures for catching and holding small fish, thereby earning another nickname, the "sawbill."

The distinctive white blaze behind the eye of the male may be visible as either a rectangular patch or a massive white area depending on whether the crest is lowered or elevated. They begin to pair up in mid-winter; therefore, there is a great amount of courtship of the females and rivalry between males on the ponds. It is amusing to observe the males raise and lower the white hoods as they signal rivals, and dash about in pursuit of one another. The male gives every sign of strutting before the hens—is it possible for a duck to strut in the water? In any event he shows himself in the best possible light in hopes the lovely female will choose him as her mate before they all leave in May for the breeding grounds in our northern states and Canada. There, they nest in tree cavities in wooded areas near rivers and small lakes—much the same terrain they have chosen on Kiawah for the winter.

Alligators probably take a few of these ducks but the birds do not seem to be frightened off a pond by the presence of alligators. In fact, ducks of several species have been observed resting and feeding within a few yards of alligators on the banks. When alligators or otters are present in the water, ducks keep a wary eye on them and move out of the way but seldom take flight. Bobcats, eagles and some of the larger hawks are other natural predators that the ducks have always had to avoid. The human predator, the poacher, was present on the island as recently as the 1980s but did not seem to reduce the population significantly.

It is encouraging that some species are becoming habituated to human disturbance. Some may disappear due to reduction in their numbers nationwide or be too shy to tolerate the human activity on Kiawah, but others will continue to return and add beauty and vitality to our ponds.

Cougar, Are You Really Here Too?

*S*oftly, like a whisper in the night, it creeps in and out of our South-ern psyche. It's the stuff legends are made of. Elusive and mysterious, the graceful eastern cougar has existed more in our minds, imaginations, tales and fables than in real-ity. Or has it?

This is the way an article on the cougar was begun by Pris Massenburg of the Nongame and Heritage Trust of our state wildlife department. An animal of the western hemisphere, the cougar was one of the first New World animals recorded by explorers, and was common throughout the continental United States. It is still fairly common in the West, but in the East it is known to exist only in southern Florida. Although, it could exist almost anywhere in the country that offers sufficient prey and adequate cover. Its food of choice is deer, so it should find Kiawah, with its large population of deer, quite acceptable.

Cougars are so secretive, so rare and wander over an area so great that the chances of seeing one are slim even if it does pass through the island. If you happen to see an animal with a long tawny buff or reddish brown body, a creamy white belly, a long dark-tipped tail and small head with rounded ears, then indeed you might be seeing a cougar. An adult can attain a length of 7 feet, including a tail extending perhaps 3–4 feet. It may weigh as much as 120–150 pounds, although a smaller one of half that weight is quite possible. (By comparison, our Bobcat has a body length of 3 feet and weight of only 20 pounds.)

Despite the poor odds of seeing this cat, the state wildlife department does get reported sightings each year, and I frequently receive reports of sightings of what would appear to be a cougar on this island. But does this cat really visit Kiawah? SC Dept. of Natural Resources personnel inform me that only a photograph, a paw print or a scat (feces) will be acceptable evidence, short of a road-kill.

A good photograph will be great if we can only arrange an appointment between the cat and the photographer with his paraphernalia in place and the sun shining brightly. In lieu of that, a paw print would be nice but the animal typically walks on logs, meanders back and forth along the edge of roads and avoids wet or muddy spots. Why would a collection of scat be acceptable? Like most cats, cougars groom themselves frequently by licking their fur. The loose hair is ingested, passes out in the feces, and the modern analytical laboratory can readily distinguish hair of that species, the long awaited cougar.

So, I can do no better than again quote Pris Massenburg, *A solitary animal, so secretive and silent afoot, does it walk among us like a ghost in the night?*

Winter, 1995

The Striped
Dolphin

One of my concerns on the beach, aside from the turtle nesting program in the summer, is keeping a record of marine mammals that become stranded on the Kiawah beach. A dolphin or whale that washes ashore may be dead or it may be injured or sick. If it is alive, I must inform state and federal agents promptly so that rescue operations can be initiated as soon as possible. If the animal is dead, I need to identify the species and sex, take body measurements and note any physical injuries that might indicate the cause of death.

On New Year's Day, a dead dolphin washed ashore. It was quite different from the Bottlenose dolphins that cruise along our shoreline and in the Kiawah River. The slender female was beautifully patterned on the dorsal surface with stripes of dark blue and white and the ventral surface was white. She was further set off from the Bottlenose by a slender beak with 44 pairs of tiny sharp teeth in both upper and lower jaws. By contrast, the Bottlenose has only half that number of larger teeth.

After rummaging through my guide, *Marine Mammals Ashore*, I thought I could identify the animal as the Striped dolphin (*Stenella coeruleoalba*). The species name *coeruleo* translates as "sky blue" and *albus* of course is "white." I soon learned that this was only the second observation of the Striped dolphin in the state of South Carolina. The first stranding of the species had occurred at Sullivan's Island in May of 1976. Therefore, my identification was greeted with considerable skepticism. Wayne McFee of the Charleston Laboratory of the National Marine Fisheries Service collected the skull for study of the bone configurations and took tissue samples for DNA comparisons. Only much later was I able to give a sigh of relief; my identification was confirmed.

This pelagic species of dolphin occurs in temperate and tropical oceans around the world, where the animals feed on small fish, squid and shrimp. They seldom enter coastal waters, but if they do, the entire school may panic as a result of some disturbance and strand in large numbers. Under normal circumstances, they are a gregarious lot and travel in schools of several hundred. Observers report that about one-third of the school will be in the air at one time as they make spectacular leaps, with mothers and calves jumping in unison.

The one on our beach bore no marks of injury; probably she weakened from disease, fell behind the others and died alone. Because of the cold weather, she was not torn apart by sharks and so came onto our beach. These bits and pieces that wash up on our shore are but a tantalizing hint of the wonders out there beneath the waves. It must be a splendid sight to be on shipboard and watch several Striped dolphins ride the bow wave in clear tropical waters while others leap toward the sun in spectacular arcs of coeruleoalba.

Dead Trees Can Be A Valuable Part of Your Landscape

The managers and maintenance workers on both golf course and community association property are well aware of the value of dead trees, and they seldom take one down unless it is necessary. Property owners often will leave such a tree in place, but with the intention of removing it later when landscaping plans solidify. By then, they have become attached to the indefinable beauty of the tree, especially an oak with its sculptural angularity like a Giacometti or the reclining massiveness of a piece by Henry Moore. The roughly textured bark overlain with lichens resembles the hide of an ancient alligator in its varied shades of gray, and the draperies of Spanish moss and Resurrection fern render each piece a priceless lawn sculpture created and decorated in Nature's unique way.

The miniature garden of ferns is both a rain gauge and a haven for small plants and animals. The Resurrection fern acquired its name from the habit of its fronds to curl up during a drought with the gray lower surface outward, giving it the appearance of being dead. But the frond absorbs water quickly after a rain, and presto, it uncurls and becomes as alive and green as ever. Whether wet or dry, the fern garden provides a shelter for the Carolina anole. This little lizard, so common to the low country, matches its color to conform to that of the fronds that conceal it. It will be a light emerald green if the garden is damp and dull olive brown or gray if the fronds are shriveled and dry.

Once you have found your private little garden, you might wish to explore it for the Green-fly orchid that sometimes grows there. It is the only epiphytic orchid that can survive north of Florida, and it will be difficult to locate for its elliptic (lanceolate) leaves are even smaller than the fern fronds. In July, you might be fortunate enough to see blooms on the orchid, and the tiny yellow-green flowers may linger until December.

The birds and animals attracted to those old trees are added sources of entertainment throughout the year. We all know that woodpeckers need dead trees to provide hollow cavities for nesting and roosting, as well as a food depot of insects and other invertebrates. Depending on the type of wood and the extent of decay, a woodpecker can chisel out a nest cavity in days or perhaps weeks. But often a Pileated woodpecker will take the easy way. It will tap to locate a preexisting hollow cavity, and then merely knock in one or more entrances and exits.

Only when these birds encounter a shortage of dead trees are they likely to explore the possibilities of using the side of your home. Indeed, homeowners who spare one of these old trees may ward off a number of potential wildlife problems. Bats, raccoons and squirrels are notorious for getting into attic spaces, and by providing a natural abode for these critters, you may dissuade them from invading your own home.

Most occupants of tree cavities are secondary users, that is, they cannot excavate a cavity of their own but must rely on one of the woodpeckers to hollow out their new home. More than two dozen species of birds are known to use these nest cavities. These include such backyard favorites as bluebirds, wrens, titmice, and chickadees.

Given the right conditions these trees can support one of our most engaging urban cavity-dwellers, the Eastern Screech owl. Only 8 to 10 inches tall, it is our smallest "eared" owl and can easily fit itself and family into a woodpecker cavity. Its name is somewhat misleading, because it does not screech. Its call is a wavering, tremulous cry that may enter your window during the night more like an eerie, ghostly echo. The fluffy little owl lives year-round on Kiawah, and it may lay 4 or 5 white eggs in a tree cavity around February. The baby screech owls will remain in the nest until they are about a month old; then the parents begin their hunting lessons for mice, voles, snakes and an occasional small bird.

All of these secondary occupants are indebted to the homeowner for leaving the tree standing and to the woodpeckers for excavating the cavities. Man-made bird houses, bat boxes and squirrel boxes can help ease the wildlife housing shortage, but these should be considered supplements rather than substitutes. Somehow, there's nothing like the real thing.

The Pygmy Sperm Whale

On the Sunday following the appearance of the Striped dolphin, a live Pygmy Sperm whale was left stranded in front of the Beach Club as the tide receded. By the time I arrived in the early afternoon Tom Murphy of the S.C. Dept. of Natural Resources had been notified and was on his way from his home at Green Pond. Meanwhile, concerned beach-walkers and staff from the Beach Club clustered around the stricken animal, tablecloths from the Club were draped over it and volunteers had formed a bucket brigade to keep the animal wet. It was far from the best of times to be on the beach, for the day was raw with a cold, wet wind off the water. However, the low black clouds, wind whipped surf and long skeins of ducks flying low over the water added to the excitement and beauty of the scene—if one were warm enough to appreciate it all.

Upon the arrival of Tom Murphy, the tempo immediately increased. A stretcher quickly was placed beside the whale, and the animal was rolled onto it with the aid of many eager hands. I noted that Tom wore long, heavy gloves, and I hope the others washed promptly and thoroughly. In an earlier article concerning another whale that stranded in August of 1994, I cautioned that these marine mammals that strand usually are dying, and some of their diseases are transmissible to humans. Anyway, the animal on the stretcher was lifted into the back of Tom's truck by eight or nine of us and away Tom went toward the laboratory at Fort Johnson.

By then, the kitchen staff of the Club had sent out a large thermos of hot chocolate, that was greatly appreciated by all of us before we scattered for warmth and shelter. And when I closed the gate and left five minutes after the departure of the whale, the wintry beach was devoid of life except for those lonely gulls that call it home.

At Fort Johnson, the decision was made to euthanize the animal because of its poor condition. During the next day, Wayne McPhee of the National Marine Fisheries Service did an autopsy. It was a young male only 8.3 feet in length, heavily loaded with internal parasites and with an enlarged and abnormally shaped heart. Laboratory reports on analysis of tissue samples later may reveal other abnormalities in this unfortunate animal that beached itself to die despite the kindly efforts of all those concerned folks.

The Great Horned Owls Had Severe Loses in This Winter's Nesting

Great Horned owls are unusual birds, because they nest in the winter. This year I became aware of three nestings, and all were beset with difficulties. The first nest was one that had been built by ospreys just west of Willet pond. In mid-January I noted that an owl was incubating her eggs there. After 34 days, the owl began sitting higher in the nest as though the eggs had hatched and she was brooding the chicks. This was right on time; the incubation period for the species is reported to be 26–35 days.

The big nest was quite dilapidated when the owl appropriated it in January, for it had been neglected since the osprey family left last July. As time went by during the present occupancy by the owl family, deterioration continued for owls are notoriously poor housekeepers. In this case, the owls paid the price. During the bitter cold spell early in March the owl was unable to shield the chicks from the frigid winds out of the north that surged through the flimsy structure. They perished.

I was aware of the loss on the morning that the parent failed to be at the nest, and then I saw the pale body of at least one chick in the nest. The following day the nest was truly abandoned; some scavenger, probably a crow or vulture, had removed the carcass. I walked out to the base of the tall pine tree that contained the nest, but a thorough search of the densely overgrown area failed to reveal chicks, living or dead. The adult owls were not seen again at the nest, and it is highly unlikely that they would attempt to renest so late in their season. Not all is lost, however, for the ospreys have reclaimed the nest—but that is another story.

On February 16th, I was informed by Bill Pence of the second Great Horned owl nest, located high in a pine tree between their home and the 7th tee of Turtle Point golf course. When I first viewed it, the owls had two fluffy chicks in the nest that Redtailed hawks had built and successfully used for several years. On March 4th, only one chick could be seen in the nest, and Cathy Pence informed me later that the other chick was in her backyard. Sure enough it was crouched there, all fluffed up, and looking very belligerent as I approached. I picked it up with great care not to be exposed to its threatening beak and talons, but only later did I realize that I had neglected the greater menace. I had been doing all this with my back to the parent owl watching from the nest above. Fortunately she did not choose to employ her own weapons on my exposed rear.

After it was decided that restoration of the chick to the nest was too dangerous an undertaking, I passed the chick to Dennis Bernard, a member of our rescue team for injured birds. He in turn relayed it to the Charleston Raptor Center. There, Jim Elliott found the chick to be in very good condition and placed it in the hacking program. Hacking is now a rather common and quite successful procedure for restoring chicks and injured birds to the wild. It is done in this way. An elevated shelter for the bird is closed on three sides and fitted with bars on the fourth side. A nest is formed inside the box and the chick is placed within it. Feeding is done surreptitiously so that the chick does not form an attachment for the humans. Once the chick devel-

43

ops to the stage of fledging, the bars are removed and the bird is on its own.

The second chick in the original nest continued to develop nicely. Its progress was followed by the golfers and some even added binoculars to their golf bags. By the end of March, both chick and parent were edging out onto branches beside the nest. Even the parent was clumsy in walking, and it occurred to me that owls really don't walk much as they go about their business. The chick was especially uncertain and several times I held my breath for fear it would topple as it teetered along the branch like a sleepwalker. On the first of April the chick left the nest and was seen in the top of a nearby pine tree. There, it was mobbed by a flock of crows, a rude introduction to the real world. Now, will the Redtailed hawks finally reclaim their old nest?

The third nest is surrounded with the greatest degree of mystery. Barbara Rooney told me in mid March that Great Horned owls had taken over another Redtailed hawk nest, this one on Ruddy Turnstone St. She had called me because there was one half-grown owl chick dead at the base of the nest tree as well as a number of feathers from some other bird. (Barbara had reported about 20 feathers, but by the time I arrived most of them had been appropriated by children for Indian headdresses). I retrieved one feather that had come from the tail of a Redtailed hawk, and I sent the carcass of the owl chick to the Charleston Raptor Center. There, it was carefully examined, and the only injuries found were internal ones associated with the fall from the nest.

Those are the facts, and there the mystery remains. Did the hawk try to repossess its rightful nest and in the scuffle was the chick knocked from the nest? Did the parent owl then kill and pluck the hawk at the nest? These mysteries add the spice to studies of wildlife on the island.

Spring, 1996

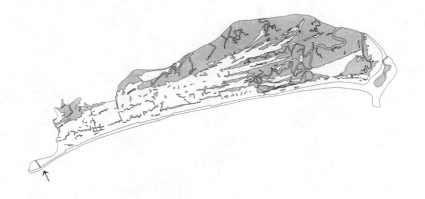

Changes at Captain Sam's Inlet This Spring

A series of charts dating back to 1661 show a pattern of reoccurring changes at the western end of Kiawah Island. Prevailing currents carry sand along the beach from east to west, the sand is deposited at the west end, and the course of the Kiawah River is deflected toward Seabrook Island. Periodically, storm waves cut through this narrow tongue of sand and reestablish the outlet of the river approximately at the position of Captain Sam's Creek. (Refer to the arrow in the illustration on the preceding page.) The sand that is liberated from Kiawah by this relocation of the river channel gradually moves further west and temporarily renourishes the beach of Seabrook Island. Then the entire process is slowly repeated.

In 1983, the developers of Kiawah and Seabrook Islands jointly agreed to accelerate these natural changes by digging a new channel for the river. The new channel cut off the end of Kiawah Island in the same location as earlier storms had done, and relocation of the inlet accomplished the same effects as nature's way.

This year property owners of Seabrook Island wish to repeat the procedure in order to liberate another million or more cubic yards of sand for renourishment of their beach. An agreement for excavation of the new channel at the same location was reached between the Town of Kiawah Island, Kiawah Resort Associates and the Town of Seabrook Island. Then Seabrook property owners contracted to have the work done at a cost of about half a million dollars. A 250-foot wide channel was to be dug to a depth of 10 feet below mean sea level. Some of the excavated sand was to be used for construction of a 2500-foot dike across the old riverbed to a height of 10 feet above mean sea level and with a width of 100 feet at the crest. A bewildering variety of huge excavating and earth moving machinery arrived and in 5 or 6 weeks, the new channel was excavated. Sand dikes were installed during the work at both the river and ocean ends to prevent premature flooding of the excavation.

Weather was perfect on the big day for opening the channel on April 4th, and a full moon guaranteed maximal tidal excursions. As the tide began to recede at 8 AM, the hefty machines started to remove the sand dike on the ocean side of the new channel and at the same time they followed the tide down the beach extending the channel for the river outflow. By some miracle, the frenetic activity of all those excavators, scraper pans, bulldozers and dump trucks in that confined space did not lead to collisions, and the sand seemed to melt away. Toward mid-afternoon some of the excavated sand was heaped into a temporary dike about half way down the beach so that more time could be obtained for removal of the last sand in advance of the incoming tide.

Flooding of the channel had been scheduled by the engineers for 7:00 PM, but the rising tide rescheduled it for 6:30. I had walked along the channel bank to view the dike at the other end. The channel already contained about a foot of water because the pumps had been withdrawn, and groundwater was seeping in on all sides. A bulldozer was whittling down the dike beside the riverbank, and opportunistic Laughing gulls were there in droves. They were feasting on the worms and crustaceans turned up by the blade of the machine, and the scene was reminiscent of the classic tableau of birds following the farmer as he prepared his field.

Returning to the more serious matter at hand, I noted several silvery trickles of water entering the channel from the dark base of the dam. Ominous! The drivers of the machines at the other end might be in for a rude shock if suddenly the river swept through the dike and rushed down its new course. However, the surprise was to come from the rising tide. By the time I was half way back to the beach, I saw the temporary dike begin to melt and the white foam of breaking waves appeared at the top. The drivers saw this at the same moment. Turning their vehicles, they raced for the security of the higher beach. Accustomed to watch the slow progression of a rising tide on the beach, I was totally unprepared for the powerful rush of water up the beach. It struck the remnants of the old dike, cut numerous ravines through it and surged down the length of the channel.

Success! In the euphoria of the moment, there was much handshaking and backslapping among the drivers, contractors and engineers. Even we spectators were shouting and gesturing as though somehow we too had participated in this engineering feat. By some minor miracle, no one was caught on a collapsing bank and precipitated into the surging torrent. Toward sunset, some of the equipment partially breached the other dike and the river turned in its new direction to meet the incoming tide. By the next day, the river current had scoured out its new bed and was busy smoothing out the banks.

What will be the consequences of this change, aside from the renourishment of the Seabrook beach? The Kiawah beach and the marsh along the river should not be affected for the ocean and river currents will continue their normal flow from east to west. People will view the long stretch of inviting beach beyond the new outlet of the river and will be tempted to wade across at low tide. This would be dangerous, for the river runs strong and swift beneath the placid surface, and often deep gullies are created in its bed. In the past people have attempted to cross that inlet, been swept out to sea and drown. So leave the inlet to the dolphins; we can always watch their antics from the security of our side of the river.

Shorebirds normally nest at the west end of Kiawah, and these include oystercatchers, willets and Wilson's plovers. Probably they will adjust to the changes quite easily. The most interesting species to observe will be the Least terns, which are classified as threatened in the state. They traditionally have nested in a colony beyond the new channel, and the birds will be arriving in May. It will be intriguing to see their reaction to the change. Perhaps they may find the broad, elevated surface of the new dike across the old river bed to their liking and establish the colony there. Watch for them!

How About
Those Squirrels
in Our Yards?

Our squirrels are too lively and mischievous to be ignored. Often as homeowners we either love them or hate them and sometimes our feelings are a love/hate mixture, but few of us can completely ignore them. They can be aggressive, destructive, obtrusive and persistent pests. Most of these conflicts center around the birdbaths and feeders. The homeowner intends them for the birds; but the squirrels (as well as the raccoons) act on the philosophy "first come first serve." At the same time, they are graceful, intelligent, inquisitive and skillful. All of these traits place them among the most interesting wildlife that we can observe right around our homes.

They are the Eastern Gray squirrels, *Sciurus carolinensis*. This is one of the most descriptive and suitable scientific names for a species that I have come across. *Sciurus* is Greek for "animal that sits in the shade of its own tail;" isn't it amazing how much information the Greeks could squeeze into seven alphabetical letters? The species name *carolinensis* signifies that the animal was first observed and named in the Carolinas.

Squirrels are classified as Rodentia or gnawing mammals, and, surprisingly, they must gnaw on hard and tough foodstuffs just to survive. The upper and lower pairs of incisor teeth are arc-shaped and chisel-edged, well adapted for cutting and gnawing food, but the incisors are rootless and grow continuously. Without constant wear the incisors would become too long and soon would prevent the animal from feeding.

Squirrels dine on a varied diet of nuts, berries, seeds, and new twigs as well as occasional insects and birds eggs. The fall crop of acorns from the oaks is their main food through the winter. These they cache in shallow cavities in the ground for consumption through the winter. For a long time, it was though that the squirrel remembered where it has buried each nut for later retrieval. More recent studies have shown that they recover buried nuts by their keen sense of smell, not by memory; and the squirrel that retrieved the nut usually was not the same one that buried it. If the winter is severe or the acorn crop small, squirrels do have alternatives besides your bird feeder. For example, I know that they feed avidly on the new growth on wax myrtles along our lagoon bank in early spring.

Few things in nature are as marvelous as a squirrel's tail, and each squirrel displays it as though proudly aware of that fact. The tail is an all-purpose appendage; a balance pole in climbing, a scarf on cold days, a semaphore flag in communication and even a parachute if the squirrel misses a branch. When marking its territory, a squirrel flicks its tail in an arpeggio of twitches, then moves a few feet up the tree trunk or along the branch and signals again. And when two squirrels meet communication relies mainly on the vigorous semaphore signals of the two tails. During a rain, squirrels fold their tails up over their heads as umbrellas. When cold, they wrap up in them or place them around small offspring.

Gray squirrels cannot be differentiated as to sex either by color or size. However, during mating season in mid-winter and again in early summer the female is easily identified. When a female squirrel is in estrus, she exudes a volatile hormone that is irresistible perfume for all the male squirrels in the neighborhood. Then you will be able to distinguish the female, for she will be leading the pack of lusting males is a wild chase—waltzing about the yard—swirling around tree trunks—teetering on the ends of branches—making daring leaps to neighboring trees—and then down to do it all over again. And squeaking in excitement all the while. In this fashion she tests her suitors for speed, agility and persistence.

Finally, she accepts one male. After that brief encounter, the male leaves her fully responsible for the pregnancy and its aftermath, as he tears off in search of another female. He leaves secure in the knowledge that no subsequent male will have access to the first one, because during the copulation he has secreted a wax plug which blocks the female's vagina and prohibits further breeding. (How do biologists *know* these things?) The pregnant female becomes solitary, increasingly territorial, and chases away all other squirrels from the den tree chosen for her nest. She would prefer to nest in a tree cavity, but if none is available she will build a bulky leaf nest usually toward the top of a tree.

About 44 days after fertilization, the female gives birth to a litter of three to five young. They are about four inches long, naked and blind, but after only a week on the mother's milk they double in weight. When their eyes finally open at five weeks, they are fully covered with fur and measure about ten inches overall. The mother never brings solid food to the young in the nest, but as those remarkable incisors are coming through the gums the babies start to nibble on anything within reach. That includes insects that venture close to the nest, and sometimes even their litter-mates! At ten weeks, baby squirrels are weaned, and with those developing teeth, you can scarcely blame the mother. Thereafter, they fend for themselves on a diet of solid foods, because their mother has again been the target of another chase through the treetops by a throng of eager males. Busy preparing herself and a nest for the summer litter, she has no further concern for her first born.

Completely on their own, the youngsters stay together as they learn the hard lessons of the world. Their keen sense of smell permits them to find acorns buried during the winter by older squirrels and they sample every sort of insect and plant. At this time they are highly vulnerable to predators—quite aside from our cars and trucks that certainly take their toll. These many predators include hawks and owls, bobcats, foxes, raccoons, snakes and even herons. (One winter I observed a Great Blue heron in the horrendous process of swallowing a squirrel head first. You should not dwell on this gustatory feat, but I do think the unfortunate squirrel was dead at the time.) Predation is so heavy on these youngsters that their estimated average lifetime is only one year despite the fact that they are capable of living as long as 20 years in captivity.

But they are so lively and obsessed with each other that they cannot take life too seriously. I have seen them roll about together on the ground like kittens. And at other times they play complicated games of tag by the hour on the large branches and in the crotches of the great oak outside the window of my study. So, if occasionally you are irritated by their antics, try to be sympathetic. They have only a few days, and they must live them to the fullest.

Nature's Way of Handling A Superabundance of Pine Voles

Pine voles, also called Woodland voles, are short-tailed rotund little rodents that occur throughout the Low Country. On Kiawah Island, the numbers of these mice fluctuate widely, and this spring there has been a population explosion. The voles are everywhere! Even bikers must be cautious, for voles scurry across the paths as though bent upon suicide beneath the wheels. Therefore, I hear many vole stories in these days of abundance. One of these by Stan Novaco, who lives on Augusta National Ct., nicely illustrates both the probably origin of the problem and one solution to it, but first my admonishment. We property owners are in large measure responsible for this abundance. On the one hand, we cover large areas of the island with pine straw which is ideal protective cover for the voles, and we import onto the island daily probably hundreds of new voles in the huge truckloads of pine straw. On the other hand, many of us (but not Stan) seize every opportunity to kill the non-poisonous snakes that normally control the vole population. End of sermonette, let Stan relate his story:

"While spreading pine straw, I heard rustling in the stack of bales. In quick succession a large vole (assumed to be mom) and 3 smaller baby voles popped out of different holes between the bales. One of the babies was followed by a yellow and brown snake about 2 feet long (later identified as a non-poisonous rat snake). The snake soon had the baby wrapped in its coils while it kept its head out in a defensive posture. The baby squealed and the mommy vole made a couple of threatening passes at the snake, never getting too close. Soon she and the remaining babies returned to the cover of the bales.

"The snake by this time had become an almost round ball around the captured vole, and the snake's head was somewhere inside the ball. Later as the snake began to straighten out all that was evident of the vole was a lump behind the snake's head with two small feet and the tail sticking out of its mouth. Soon these too disappeared as the lump moved slowly toward the middle of the snake. The snake, lump and all, moved into denser vegetation and soon disappeared from view.

"At one time while I was watching the snake I thought I saw the large vole run across the lawn to the cover of some holly. There appeared to be something in her mouth. After the snake moved off, I decided to watch the other side of the bale pile where I thought I had seen the vole originate her trip across the lawn. Soon I saw her coming out of the holly toward the bale pile. Although I did not hear a sound, one of the babies came out of the pile to meet her. I was not close enough to see what she was doing, but she appeared to be holding the baby between her paws. As I moved in to get a closer look, she moved off toward the holly bush with most of her baby inside her mouth. Now I know why some people think rodents eat their young."

An increase in the number of predators is Nature's way of controlling these population explosions. In addition to the usual predators such as Stan's snake, hawks, owls, foxes and bobcats, some opportunistic wildlife species are helping to reduce the vole inundation. Some of these are quite unexpected, for example, I recently was informed that even the Common egrets and Great Blue herons are enjoying the abundance of voles.

Summer, 1996

The Glass Lizard, An Animal in Transition

T oo frequently in our warm summer months, an unusual sort of animal may be found in gutters that border our roads. Surprisingly, it is trapped there despite the shallowness of the gutters. Most of you upon a casual glance would think it is some sort of snake that may have been killed by a passing car. Not so, it a curious form of lizard that has chosen to dispense with legs—a glass lizard. The one on Kiawah is the Eastern glass lizard (*Ophisaurus ventralis*). I fancy that it acquired the name glass lizard because it, like most lizards, will break off its tail when under the stress of pursuit and capture.

Until one of them makes the mistake of attempting to cross a road, it is not likely that you will see it, because glass lizards live in burrows that they can dig in the sandy soil. Also, they are usually out and about in weedy areas near the ponds and marshes only in the early morning or late in the hours of dusk. Gliding through the jungle of dense vegetation, they hunt insects, the smaller lizards and snakes, and will take the eggs of birds that nest on the ground. If you examine one unfortunate enough to end up in one of our gutters, you will see that it is speckled greenish-brown, completely lacking even the vestige of legs and with the slinky sinuous shape we associate with snakes. The reported length is from 18 to 42 inches although those I see on Kiawah are near the 18-inch mark.

Strangely enough, while true snakes seem to have no difficulty passing over these shallow gutters, the glass lizard cannot get sufficient traction and will die of dehydration in the hot sun unless rescued. Whenever I encounter one in such a predicament, I use the toe of my shoe to nudge it gently over the gutter. Then it swirls off through the grass at top speed. If you wish to pick it up, grasp it firmly behind the head for it is harmless. However, in all likelihood it will thrash about so violently that you will drop it. In the struggle, it probably will cast off the last few inches of its tail that will writhe about on its own for some time. As I think about it, probably you should leave it on the ground and just nudge it along.

I didn't follow my own advise on a pleasant Sunday morning this May when I plucked a glass lizard from a gutter along Bufflehead Dr. It was writhing and coiling around my forearm in a snaky fashion just as a car approached with two couples who were obviously visitors just back from church and taking a lovely Sunday drive. As the car slowly passed, all four faces were pressed to the windows. It stopped and the four faces swiveled back to watch me release the lizard in the grass. Then we went our separate ways, but I feel certain that the four had a revised impression of the Island of Kiawah.

In late spring, the female glass lizard will deposit anywhere from 5 to 17 eggs, usually in a shallow depression under a moss-covered log or similar secret place. She remains protectively coiled around her eggs until they hatch and actually incubates them in a sense, for she warms her body in the sun and then returns to transfer the warmth to the eggs. When the hatchling emerges from the egg it is only 7 inches long, but it must immediately set off to make its own way in this world.

Two other species, the Slender and Island glass lizards are common in the state, and several other species of legless lizards are known in other parts of the world. It is intriguing to me why a four-legged animal would evolve in such a fashion as to abandon its legs. Herpetologists who are paid to worry about such matters suggest that benefits from ease of burrowing justify the loss. A human would not dream, even in a worst nightmare, that loss of limbs would be beneficial in any evolutionary sense. But for the lizard with its long slender body already close to the ground, the loss of limbs might be no big deal. It could slip through the tangle of weeds quite nicely and slither into its burrow free of the encumbrance of those pesky legs.

To continue this evolutionary train of thought further; it is believed that snakes probably evolved from an early species of lizard that had dispensed with legs. However, modern snakes do have the advantage over the glass lizard that they can cope with Kiawah gutters. Both lizards and snakes have scaly skin, but the scales of snakes are larger and play an essential role in their locomotion. Snakes make use of various groups of scales to propel themselves along. For instance, when progressing in a straight line the snake uses its ventral scales by moving them forward in a continuous series of waves and hitching their edges over irregularities, then using this grip it pulls itself along by muscular effort. At any given time, several adjacent scales will be moving forward, while others will be pulling, so the general impression is of a smooth gliding motion. In climbing, the ventral scales at the lower portion of the body serve to anchor the snake as it extends the upper portion forward. When the scales in this upper region have obtained a firm grip, the rest of the body and tail are drawn up and the process is repeated.

Until our glass lizards make that next evolutionary step and develop more useful scales, let's help them out of the gutter with a gentle nudge.

Why Are We Wiring Turtle Nests?

Those of you who walk the beach during turtle nesting season may have been puzzled last summer to note thermocouple wires protruding from some of the nests. An explanation is needed. It all has to do with the sex ratio of the hatchlings. If you can recall your introductory biology course, you may remember that most animal species are reproduced in a 1:1 ratio of males to females by the mathematical odds of the pairing of X and Y sex chromosomes. Some reptiles, including alligators and some species of turtles, lack that pair of chromosomes and the temperature of the embryo during incubation determines sex.

A critical value, termed the Pivotal temperature, is the temperature that will yield equal numbers of male and female hatchlings. The Pivotal temperature is close to 84° F. for Loggerhead turtles that nest on beaches along the southeastern coast of the United States. Any departure from that temperature will alter the sex ratio; higher temperatures favor females and lower temperatures favor males.

Any marked skewing of the ratio in favor of either sex by an unfavorable nest temperature might threaten the long-term survival of the nesting rookery, and this is of concern to those of us interested in preservation of the species. The millions of years of survival would suggest that the turtles had adjusted to everything from glacial cooling to global warming and drastic changes in sea level. Always they have found suitable beaches to keep the sex ratio in balance. However, the arrival of mankind may limit their ability to make those adjustments, either by denying them access to suitable beaches, or by well-meaning persons relocating nests to regions at improper temperatures.

Without trying to draw too much from the 1995 season on the Kiawah beach, the temperature data suggested that the sex ratio for hatchlings coming off our beach was close to the ideal 1:1 ratio. By contrast, hatchlings from the cooler beaches of North Carolina are predominantly male while those to the south in Florida are mostly female. Therefore, we are fortunate to have a beach with a favorable summertime temperature for the turtle nests. To reassure ourselves that these conditions persist, it seems prudent that we continue to have thermocouple wires sticking up through the sand in the summer.

Life and Death
at the Pond's Edge

We have two species of aquatic birds on many of our ponds that I am sure a number of you mistake for ducks. Both birds have chicken-like beaks so unlike the duck's bill that you quickly should see your error. Beyond the possession of similar beaks, however, the two birds are quite different. The small dove-gray Pied-billed grebe is a diving and swimming bird with feet placed far to the rear like the closely related loon. I hope to describe it in detail later, for it has several entertaining traits.

The one on today's menu (and it will soon be apparent why I introduce it in such a curious fashion) is the Common gallinule (*Gallinula chloropus*), sometimes called the Moorhen. It is an amphibious bird that displays the contrasting faces of Janus; sometimes it resembles a duck and at other times a chicken. Paddling along in the water, it has the look of a duck for its neck is retracted and the long legs are hidden beneath the water. It is the one that is dark blue—almost black—with a white stripe along the side and a white patch on the rump. The definitive feature is the bright red frontal plate that terminates in the yellow beak.

When the gallinule emerges from the water and is running along the vegetation or resting on the bank it transforms into a tall, thin rail. It has the appearance of a young chicken—what we Kansans called a Spring chicken—all legs and neck with a narrow body in between.

I was particularly aware of this contrast when I had occasion to see several together beside a pond early in June. I warn you, it was not a pleasant viewing. I was biking across a short bridge over the pond when I noticed a mother gallinule and her three youngsters on the bank just ahead. The three juveniles were nearly as tall as the mother but even thinner, a smoky blue-gray overall except for a shading into subdued tan on breast and belly. All four were pacing about in a most agitated fashion and looking intently down into the water.

Following their gaze, I saw a large alligator floating close to the pond's edge and with a fourth young gallinule between its jaws. Gallinules are noted for making a variety of strange calls, but this distressed mother gave forth a dreadfully drawn-out, doleful sort of moaning call that I had never heard on any other occasion. Then, not once but three times the alligator would surge toward the bank and open its jaws to more fully display its mangled victim, before it disappeared beneath the murky surface. The reptile was clearly taunting the poor family pacing about and so distraught that they had not even noticed my arrival. This is the first time I have ever seen an animal display one of those base traits that we usually attribute only to primates and *Homo sapiens* in particular.

Turning to more happy times in the lives of this family, the nesting probably began in early May. The mated pair usually construct the nest in the thickest vegetation along the bank of their pond. They use the same vegetation to construct the nest and nestle it down close to the surface of the water. Therefore, the nest and its six to twelve pale brown eggs are extremely difficult to find. To add to the camouflage, the eggs are cryptically marked with splotches of brown and gray. I have watched a mated pair come and go from a specific patch of reeds. And yet, when I approached on the bank, I could peer all about closely and not discern the nest that I knew must be there. Nevertheless, the nests are sometimes found by prowling raccoons and snakes, while crows and grackles cruising just above the reeds also take a toll.

Both parents share incubation for about three weeks, and the precocious young leave the nest soon after hatching. The pretty little things in black down, set off with red beaks, are easy prey for alligators, turtles and even the larger fish as they paddle about. It is a good thing that the adults are so prolific. Those that survive the first weeks grow rapidly, and within six or seven weeks, they are about as able as the adults to elude their enemies. However, it is not until early fall that the wings and tail are fully developed so that they can fly.

Even the adults seem reluctant to fly if other means of transportation will do. They are capable of strong, sustained flight, for those in northern climes migrate south in the winter. But a gallinule that has been disturbed on its home pond flutters along barely skimming the surface, half flying and half pattering over the pond surface, as though unable to rise. The bird seems most at ease and is most graceful when walking lightly over the matted vegetation or through the reeds probing for its food with quick, nervous jabs much after the manner of a chicken. Then, you are likely to hear clucking and chuckling sounds that might make you think a barnyard fowl had wandered into the reeds at the pond edge. Don't be surprised though if a duck sails out—a duck with the beak of a chicken.

Fall, 1996

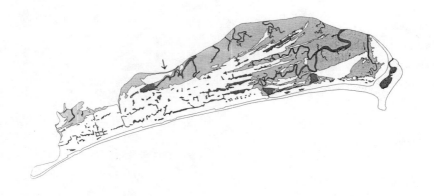

Some Vestiges of the Early Plantation Period Still Linger on Kiawah

Of the three plantation homes known to have been built on Kiawah Island, the Shoolbred home was apparently the most elegant. It was built about 1790 on what is now called Rhett's Bluff (indicated by the arrow in the illustration on the previous page.) A painting dated 1870 shows the home as it once existed, facing the Kiawah River, which was the principal route of travel at that time. From the home, curving paths led down through formal gardens to the dock and an elaborate gazebo. Sad to say, only the painting remains, for the home was destroyed by fire during the Civil War. In addition to the brick foundations of the home that are still in place, vestiges of those bygone plantation days can be found nearby. I refer to some odd cannas that now grow wild in the locality where the old home stood.

The cannas appear quite unlike those now available from nurseries and other suppliers. They are tall and green leafed, but the striking difference is the tiny brilliantly red bloom—quite different from the fleshy blossom so popular now. It is likely that the bulbs were brought over in ships from England in those early days, and carefully placed in the formal gardens of the plantation home.

Betty Stringfellow, a local resident who is writing a history of Johns Island, knows this canna lily well, for some grow in her yard. She recently told me that her great grandfather William Andell moved here from New York in 1877. At that time former slaves were returning to find their houses, like the plantation home, burned or in ruins as a consequence of the Civil War. William Andell built a number of houses for them in an area beyond the fields near Bohicket Road. Kindly man that he must have been, Mr. Andell had some of the cannas from the ruins of the Shoolbred plantation placed beside those houses as a beacon of hope in those troubled times.

Today, tomato fields have displaced both houses and cannas. However, you may see the cannas growing in profusion on lots along River Marsh Lane and New Settlement Rd at Rhetts Bluff. Also, a few are along the boardwalk over the freshwater marsh at the same location. The intense red blossom still remains as a beacon, swaying in the breeze like a flickering flame against the dark green background of dense foliage.

The blossoms are a strong enticement for the Ruby-throated hummingbirds. I know this for some of the bulbs that I transplanted along the bank of Canvasback pond behind my home are the first of my cannas to bloom in the spring and the last to fade in the fall. All through the summer the hummingbirds spend far more time visiting them than the others from the nursery with their showy flowers of multiple hues. Perhaps the colonial plants invest more in nectar and less in floral profusion.

Turtle Patrol
Happenings

Each year members of the turtle patrol encounter crises and problems beyond the call of duty, and this year was no exception. In June, the nesting patrol encountered a turtle track that led between the pontoons of a sailboat. But what's this? The track did not continue beyond the boat! Puzzled, they peered beneath it to discover the unfortunate turtle entangled in the rigging lines. They freed her by cutting a rope that bound her left front flipper; then, she crawled out and slowly started back toward the water. She must have been struggling for hours and become totally exhausted, because she required nearly one and one-half hours to make the trip. Once afloat, all flippers seemed to operate and off she went. Increasingly, the beach furniture and toys left on the beach present unnecessary hazards for these turtles that are simply trying to perform their natural duties for survival.

A team at hatching time became another rescue squad when they found ants invading a nest. Quickly digging down, they found eggs and baby turtles covered with the biting ants. Despite the ants running up their own arms and legs, the trio pulled everything out of the infested nest. Carefully they brushed off the ants (to the neglect of other ants on their own skin), and sorted through the lot to separate live hatchlings from the many that were dead or dying. The 48 intact eggs that could not be invaded by the ants were placed in one new nest, and 38 turtles still trying to struggle out of their shells were placed in a second nest. Later, a total of 61 hatchlings emerged from the two nests. These were 61 hatchlings that would never have made it without the help of this dedicated trio!

We are sometimes surprised that a few ants can kill these sturdy hatchlings. However, I dug a nest under similar circumstances on Labor Day afternoon with the unsolicited help of a holiday crowd. The next day numerous small blisters had appeared on my hands and forearms. So, think how much greater must be the toxic reaction for these tiny hatchlings!

The last nest of the season was #209 on August 18th, fully 15 days after nest #208 and long after we had ceased patrolling the beach for additional nests. Cathie McCrann was the heroine of the day. She found the crawl tracks in front of the Beach Club while on hatching patrol. Cathie called me and stood guard until I arrived; then, the two of us relocated the nest of 118 eggs to a safer spot. This is definitely Cathie's nest—I'm sure she will patrol it carefully at hatching time. We may need to guard against thermal shock at that time as the hatchlings emerge from the warm nest into the cold air of the beach in late October, but the water temperature should still be warm enough for the turtles to operate once we get them in the ocean.

Those Ospreys Are Such Unpredictable Characters!

Each year, we see more ospreys nesting on Kiawah. This is a splendid sign that our environment is healthy, that ponds are brimming with wholesome fish, and that nesting sites are a safe haven for the rearing of chicks. This year, as I observed parents and chicks at four active nests, I was especially intrigued by the differences in behavior of the various families—from nest construction right on through the final departure of the family members at the season's close. These striking variations in behavior were in marked contrast to the stereotype that we often associate with the actions of the "lower" animals. I will try to illustrate this as we go along.

To simplify description of the various nests, I will list them at the outset. Nest N-1 is a new nest, well constructed high in the uppermost crotch of a live pine tree between Bufflehead pond and the intersection of Golden Eye Drive and Bufflehead Drive. Nest N-2 is an old nest from which two chicks were taken by owls last year; it is north of the intersection of Bass Creek Lane and Ocean Course Drive. This nest, the most compact and neatest of them all, was the only one built on a dead pine snag. Unfortunately its time ran out early in October but well past the nesting season, for the branch that supported it broke off in a storm. When I checked all the nests in October, this was the only site with an osprey perched nearby. Perhaps it is one of the former owners, now in a quandary where to relocate next year.

Nest numbers N-3 through N-5 have been reserved for the three nest poles installed seven years ago and which have received scant attention from the osprey community in all that time. Oh, it is true that occasionally an osprey will drop a branch on the platform or drape a strand of Spanish moss over the side, and then perch on the edge till I come along and jump up and down with excitement. But soon the bird becomes bored with the game and flies off for more important pursuits, leaving it to the wind to sweep the platform bare once again.

Nest N-6 is a huge ramshackle affair that barely seems to cling to a crook in the trunk of a tall pine tree just west of Willet pond. Branches and debris protrude in every direction like a monstrous brown pincushion, and even a large branch broken from the tree has somehow been incorporated and sways in response to every passing breeze. Possibly the pair that built it wanted to create a distinctive new style—the casual, lived-in look. Despite its appearance, it is the nest from which two juvenile ospreys fledged last year and owls nested unsuccessfully this winter.

Nest N-7 is one new to me but well known in the osprey community for years; it is a huge, well-built nest high in a pine tree between the marsh and the new Otter Island Road. Despite its large size, it is the best-concealed nest of the lot, for it is surrounded by dense foliage of dark green pine needles at the very top of the tree. Finally, nest N-8 was never completed and is rapidly being disassembled in these windy days of fall. It may be seen to the north of Ocean Course Drive just before you reach Bass Creek Lane.

It is interesting that all of the nests are clustered within a radius of about a mile; this pattern of nesting by ospreys in loosely spaced colonies is a common occurrence. The reason is not known but may depend upon a concentration of suitable nesting trees and good sources of food in that particular area on the island.

As mentioned, nest N-1 was built just this year and at the time of construction both a pair of crows and a Redtailed hawk tried in turn to claim it. However, the ospreys that had worked so hard to construct the nest, now teamed up to drive off these brazen usurpers. Indeed, this mated pair seemed especially cooperative throughout the season, and from the time the female began to incubate eggs until the single juvenile fledged, the male took an unusually strong interest in the nest. In most cases the male loafs several trees away from the nest or may be completely absent much of the time. In this case, however, the male was usually seen perched on a branch beside the nest, and sometimes right on the rim of the nest, peering in to closely oversee the activity as the female tended eggs or fed the chick. Fidelity for the nest persisted after the juvenile fledged, because the parents and juvenile continued to converge at the nest and one or another of the parents would still place a fish within the nest for the juvenile. This continued to the point that the juvenile, distinguished by the speckled plumage on its back, was still feeding at the nest late in August; long after its cousins from the other nests were roaming far away. And often one or both parents still would be perched nearby; surely, this lucky chick had the most attentive of parents!

Nest N-2 was renovated unusually early, about the last week of February, and probably by the experienced pair that had nested there the previous year. Eggs were being incubated by the middle of March, and two juveniles fledged in mid-May. Clear winners for the osprey community! Also, that made up for the loss of their chicks to the Great Horned owls during the previous year. In contrast to the behavior of the nesting pair in N-1, once the two juveniles in N-2 fledged, the entire family departed and not once did I see an osprey near the nest for the remainder of the summer.

75

Nest N-6 started out well, but at the time eggs should have hatched the nest was vacated. I had noted at the time of mating that the female was easily identifiable by the heavy speckling of brown feathers on her breast in contrast with the white breast of the male. After the nest was abandoned, the female was seen frequently near the nest and often perched on the rim, but the male never appeared again. Perhaps the eggs failed to hatch and he moved on, or perhaps he died and the female decided to give it up in the absence of his support for the feeding. Her faithfulness to the nest with the apparent hopes for the return of the male was touching each time, over the next month, that I observed her lingering there.

As I mentioned earlier, nest N-7 was only discovered this spring when Otter Island Road was cut, and it was possible for me to get back into the dense thicket of brush and fallen trees along the marsh. The nest, in the top of a very large pine tree, is the largest osprey nest that I have seen, and it could even accommodate a pair of eagles. I estimate the nest is four feet across and three feet in depth—it would fit nicely in the bed of my little pickup truck. Quite likely the nesting pair have used it for a number of years. Despite all the activity and noise involved in grading the land, installing utilities and surfacing the new road, they reared a family of two juveniles that fledged early in July.

Despite their acceptance of all that noisy activity below the nest, which had been so tranquil in previous years, the parents were unusually intolerant of me. As soon as the one at the nest caught sight of me, standing on the road and looking up at the nest, it would begin to call loudly in an agitated fashion and fly off the nest. Frequently the second joined in from a nearby perch and the two would circle overhead calling and obviously distressed. For that reason, I restricted my visits as much as possible, for they had enough to contend with without my adding to their apprehension.

Nest N-8 was the most disappointing of them all. The osprey pair must be novices. They did not start in earnest to pile sticks in some semblance of a nest until the third week of May; by then the youngsters across the way in N-2 had already left the nest! By mid-summer the nest still was not ready for occupancy and a thunder storm blew half of it away. Nevertheless, the two continued to bring sticks and moss from time to time. Then one day, I saw the two of them perched on branches shaped like an inverted wishbone on opposite sides of the nest shambles, and I *thought* I hear the dejected bride say, "Oh Joe, I don't know, lets give it up for this season—maybe next year . . ." And I saw them no more.

New Evidence of the Travels of Loggerhead Hatchlings That Come Off Our Beach

Biologists studying juvenile Loggerhead turtles in the Mediterranean Sea recently have been startled to find from their genetic comparison that roughly half the immature turtles feeding there came from beaches of Florida, Georgia and South Carolina. Apparently the young turtles follow the Gulf Stream up the Eastern Seaboard and then travel the North Atlantic gyre, a huge circular current that carries them toward Europe. A branch of the gyre enters the Mediterranean Sea and along with it go the young turtles.

Unfortunately, the records show that many of them are hooked and perish on the longlines running out as much as 75 miles and armed with thousands of hooks. The turtles pass these terrible lines set out by fishermen all along their route in both the Atlantic Ocean and the Mediterranean Sea.

Therefore, our poor little hatchlings face a triple whammy. As though it weren't tough enough getting by the predators on our beach just to reach the water, now they must run the gauntlet of longlines in their travels, as well as the nets of the flotilla of trawlers off our beach upon their return to nest.

Winter, 1996

Spanish Moss

Much of the aesthetic appeal and charm of the Low-country derives from the moss-draped live oaks along the roadways and waterways. Spanish moss, live oaks and the animals and birds associated with them clearly belong together in the mosaic that defines this land. They form a partnership and each contributes its unique measure to the final composition. The moss depends upon the tree for support but does it no harm, small animals such as the anole finds both shelter and insects in the moss, while the chickadee often is seen searching the gray streamers for food or strands to line its nest. Some of the warblers even carry this one step further and place their nests in dense clumps of the moss.

On a pleasant day, when the moss and squirrels are fluffy and the tree trunks are a match in the warmer shades of gray, even the shadows blend into that monochromatic theme to create a placid, harmonious composition. But at other times, when moss, oak and squirrel are uniformly dark and sodden with rain, the mood changes dramatically. The lowering branches and dark shadows add to the threatening gloom, the approach of a headless horseman seems imminent and even lines of poetry by Edgar Allan Poe are brought to mind.

When summer squalls sweep through, the maritime forest gives the Lowcountry yet another look. The moss tosses and thrashes in tune with the gusts of the tempest, stretching out level when the wind holds strong, or wavering away like fluttering banners. A forest without the moss stands still in a storm and only its branches sway in response, but when moss is out there flying in the wind the forest seems vibrantly alive and all is in motion, like the roiling surface of a mountain stream.

But some storms are too violent. Hurricane Hugo was much too vigorous for these fragile plants, and one of the many disasters that distressed us all was the loss of virtually all of the Spanish moss. Then, we really missed those intangible qualities that the moss had added and most of us had taken for granted. Today the moss has returned, and this has helped heal the wounds from that terrible storm. Therefore, you might be interested to know more about this unusual plant, because it truly is extraordinary.

The name is totally deceptive. Spanish moss is not Spanish in origin; Spanish moss is not even a moss. It is a flowering plant. Difficult as it may be to conceive, it is a relative of the pineapple. Plants of this sort are termed epiphytes, plants that grow on other plants. They are quite different from parasitic plants such as mistletoe, because they are not harmful to the tree and simply depend upon it for support.

When you look carefully at a streamer of the "moss" it is easy to discern the anatomy of the individual plants. However, be cautious about handling it, for in the Lowcountry it often harbors those vicious chiggers, locally called redbugs. Each plant is made up of a single, exceedingly thin wiry stem, sometimes many feet in length, to which are attached slender leaves. The entire plant is covered with a frosting of minute scales, and these scales hide the green of the chlorophyll and give the moss its characteristic gray color. A curtain of moss is a community of these slender plants, some of them young, some of them older and all intermixed in the tangle. The tangle was reminiscent of an old Spaniard's beard, and it is believed that this was the origin of "Spanish" in the name.

In early summer, the moss produces yellowish-green flowers so tiny that you will need a hand lens to appreciate their details. These in turn develop tiny seeds with feathery floats that catch the wind for transport all about the countryside. However, the plant most commonly spreads by vegetative reproduction as strands are carried from tree to tree by wind and birds.

Epiphytes, because they lack contact with the moist soil, are highly dependent upon rainwater; therefore, they must be drought resistant and designed to collect and husband water whenever it is available. The tiny scales of Spanish moss that give it the gray color have a very important role in trapping both water and the dust particles that bear minerals and organic components necessary for growth. So, when you view our Spanish moss draped oaks, enjoy the beauty of the moss in all its seasons and moods, but at the same time remember that this plant is exquisitely designed for survival under very harsh conditions.

The
Black-backed
Gull

One raw afternoon in January, I had a rare sighting of a Black-back gull on the beach near the Ocean Course clubhouse. This species is common along the coast to the north, and it seems to be spreading farther south each winter. The gull was in the midst of a large flock of Royal terns that were loafing on the broad flat upper beach and trying to warm themselves in the weak rays of the winter sun. I was surprised that the terns accepted the gull, for in the nesting season it is a notorious predator of tern chicks.

The enormous gull looked like a vulture from a distance for it is of the same size and only the massive black back was discernible. In fact, that somber black mien has given it the nickname of the "minister gull." Upon closer inspection, its more dramatic plumage was apparent. The black back was set off from the pure white head and underparts, and it has been said to closely resemble the Bald eagle when it soars and displays that broad black back and wings in contrast with its snow-white head and tail. If you see one on our beach you will easily be able to identify it, because it is the only gull on the East Coast whose back is solid black.

The Royal terns also are worthy of your attention; they are the large white terns with orange beaks, commonly seen on our beach throughout the year. They nested on Bird Key in the Stono River until that tiny spit of sand disappeared beneath the waves in 1995. Next summer they may decide to move their rookery to our section of beach along the Stono River. They are gregarious, but nonetheless a noisy, scrappy bunch, and you will often see several of them chasing another with a fish in its bill—all of them calling lustily and having a whale of a time. Even as I watched the scene, one tern alighted on the sand and momentarily stood waving a tiny fish in its bill, as though asking for a game of pursuit. Sure enough, several accepted the challenge and off they all went out over the wave-tousled ocean screaming wildly.

Bobcat! The Quintessential Wild Creature on Kiawah

S uddenly a large furry animal bounds across the road before our startled eyes! Only after it disappears in the brush do we realize that we have briefly glimpsed the most furtive member of our wildlife community, the bobcat (*Lynx rufus*). This cat is so secretive and unpredictable that very little is known about its habits; even modern tracking and monitoring techniques have been of little help. Most of the information that is available has come from the observations of professional trappers and hunters, as well as from people that have tried unsuccessfully to make pets of the kittens of these untamable wild cats

The bobcat is the smallest of America's wild cats, but even so it is such a ferocious and powerful animal that other wildlife give it the right of way and even a large hunting dog is no match for it. Only man with his armament of guns, steel traps and packs of hunting dogs can overwhelm it; about 200 are taken each year in South Carolina by professional trappers. There is quite a bit of variation in the species, but the bobbed tail, which is universally its most characteristic trademark, provides its name. They range over most of North America from Mexico to southern Canada. In our part of the country bobcats stand 16 to 22 inches at the shoulder and weigh about 25 lb., although the males may be somewhat larger and weigh up to 35 lb. In South Carolina, they are abundant, especially on the coastal plain. To quote a SC wildlife publication, "Habitats with a good inter-spersion of forest and cleared areas support stable bobcat popu-lations." Sound like Kiawah?

Hunters often locate dens and find the kittens playing in the sunny entryway like domestic kittens in our homes. The kittens are exceptionally alert and inquisitive, pursuing everything from wind-blown leaves to incautious mice, and often they roll about in a wild melee of rough-and-tumble mock battles. The kittens are so attractive that many people have tried to rear them as pets, but unfortunately, the developing cat retains all its wild-ness even to the point of attacking its owner. It seems to have an instinct is to kill domestic cats although in at least one instance a bobcat kitten did accept a Manx cat in the home as a playmate. The Manx as you probably recall is a rather large, bob-tailed domestic cat, so perhaps it was more readily accepted by the wild kitten. The owner of the two hoped that the male domestic cat and female bobcat might mate but the affair did not develop to that extent.

In this regard, it is interesting that three matings between bobcats and domestic cats have been reported. With the increasing population of feral cats on Kiawah, this is something that might be kept in mind. In my Field Notes for the month of July in 1981, I noted that early one morning I was driving along a dirt road, then called 5-mile road, that ran along beside Can-vasback pond in the vicinity of what is now the 10th hole of the Osprey golf course. When I rounded a curve, an entirely black cat loped ahead of my vehicle for a hundred yards or more so that I had ample opportunity to study it. It was about twice the size of a domestic cat, and its proportions were much different. It had a small head, long legs and bringing up the rear was a long black tail. Was it a hybrid? Or was it just a cougar kitten?

A recent study by a team of biologists from the University of Georgia reveals that there are about two bobcats per square mile on Kiawah Island. This is twice the density normally found for bobcats on barrier islands. Therefore, we should be aware of the presence of this cat and its modus operandi. It hunts primarily at night and the prey range from grasshoppers to deer with voles, squirrels and rabbits probably the principal prey. It may bring down a fawn in spring or attack weakened deer at any season, and as mentioned earlier, it is particularly aggressive with domestic cats, (this may help reduce our population of feral cats, which in turn may save some of our birds).

Mating occurs in spring, but the time is quite variable. The female may create a den in a recess of a downed tree on one of the vacant lots or she may locate a suitable spot beneath an unoccupied house. If the house is secluded and vacant for a long period, she may find an entrance and make her den in the interior, hoping that a plentiful supply of rodents also have sought shelter. Following a gestation period of about 60 days, from one to five kittens are born. After these are weaned in another 30–40 days, she leads them out to roam and teach them the arts of hunting and other tactics for survival. During all this time, the male normally does not participate, except of course for the initial planting of seed.

The bobcat communicates via about the same range of sounds as for the domestic cat. It snarls, spits and hisses when threatened and purrs when pleased. Claims have even been made that it mews, which seems out of character for so ferocious a cat. In courtship, it may give forth strange rumbles and yowls. Perhaps it was these bizarre caterwaulings that attracted my attention once, and again I refer to my Field Notes. This time it was in October of the year 1983 and I was looking for birds on a dirt lane that ran along the western edge of Ibis pond. In the meadow overgrown with brush and myrtle where Ocean Marsh Road now leads to the Beach Club, I heard what sounded like a Great Blue heron repeatedly calling. But what an odd place for a heron!

Then the noise abruptly ceased and a large (male?) bobcat came onto the road and sat facing me about 50 yards away. For what must have been a full minute the two of us studied one another. I felt not a twinge of fear although I was totally defenseless, and the wild cat was armed with stiletto-like canine teeth that are reported to be equal in length to those in the jaws of a cougar and powerful paws encircled with long retractable claws. Had there been a contest over the right of way I would have been ripped and torn to shreds. However, it was the wild cat that conceded the road to me as it calmly arose, slipped behind a bush and immediately vanished without even the residual grin of the Cheshire cat. Only its paw prints and sitz-mark in the dust of the road remained to verify its passage.

Control of Nuisance Alligators

The alligator control program on Kiawah Island arose out of concern in 1991 for the safety of spectators at the Ryder Cup golf matches on the Ocean Course. There were perhaps a dozen alligators of 8 to 10 feet in length at the various ponds, and these often roamed from pond to pond at night. However, at the time of the golf match, the alligators were frightened by the crowds and sensibly sought shelter and seclusion in the large Ibis and Willet ponds that adjoin the course.

After the Ryder Cup match, it was realized that there should be a continued safeguard against interactions between an expanding population of people on the island, and a growing population of alligators. Today, notification of a potentially dangerous alligator or one in the wrong place can be reported to KICA Security at any hour of the day or night. Over the past four years, an average of nine alligators per year have needed to be removed. Therefore, the alligator population on the island appears to be well managed; without any threat of their extermination, and yet with prompt removal of those few that pose a threat to people.

Spring, 1997

Marsh Hawk

Those of you that spend any amount of time gazing at the Kiawah marsh are bound to see the Marsh hawk, for that is its home and it is always at home. Looking out, you may see a dark speck coming in low over the Kiawah river. On it comes and soon you can make it out as a narrow-bodied, long-tailed, wide-winged bird in an easy gliding flight, its long wings slanted slightly upward. As it circles, the white rump patch will flash and then you know that the Marsh hawk is home. It is a lazy, loafing desultory sort of flight it seems, but really full of purpose as it systematic quarters low over the marsh in search of prey. Effortlessly it seeks the mice, rats, frogs, snakes and other prey that live there. It may even circle near you, but not too near, for it like all hawks has learned to fear the gunner.

Once the quarry is sighted, the harrier hovers like a kingfisher until just the right moment to swoop down and pin the victim with its fearsome talons. Unique among the hawks, it does not depend entirely upon its eyes in the search. It has the ability to locate prey by the sound of rustling in the reeds almost as well as the owl, thus explaining its characteristic owl-like facial disk.

Also called the North American harrier, this tireless hunter spends much of the daylight hours hunting on the wing, sometimes covering up to 100 miles in a single day. When it does alight to rest or consume prey it seldom chooses a tree or bush. Usually it will stand on the ground or perch on a stump or post in the marsh.

If you are fortunate enough to see it on the perch, inspect it closely. The Marsh hawk shows a strong sexual dimorphism that is unusual in raptors. Adult males are the whitest of any of our common hawks, with black wingtips. Adult females, noticeably larger, are tawny above and buff below, and juveniles resemble the females. All ages and sexes share the distinctive bold white rump patch that I have mentioned as the best distinguishing field mark. They are ground nesters, and are known to nest in the marshes as far south as North Carolina. Those of you living on the marsh can see them frequently from your windows. Now, you might make a project of being especially watchful in the April and May period when they could surprise us and chose to nest in our southern marsh.

On the Golf Course, Not All the Drama Occurs Above Ground

L et the play begin!

SCENE 1

As the curtain rises we see the villainous Mole cricket at center stage contentedly munching a clump of lush fairway grass. Our villain resembles the common Field cricket, but it is slightly larger. It is notorious as the insect most destructive of turfgrass in the southeast, and its name arises from its habit of creating tunnels that run along the earth like tiny burrows.

Now George Frye, manager of the Ocean Golf Course, enters stage right. Suddenly, George espies the bad cricket. How can it be stopped? George has a wide spectrum of synthetic pesticides that might be used but the options are limited. Even if he selects one of the least harmful for humans, it may still injure or kill wildlife. The poisoned cricket is quite likely to die on the surface and be eaten by a gull or other bird. Slowly, the ingested toxins may accumulate and ultimately sicken or even kill the gull. As the curtain falls, we see George standing perplexed and pensive.

SCENE 2

Our hero the nematode enters stage left. Our hero does not rush on stage for it is a tiny worm accustomed to creeping slowly along between soil particles. It is S. riobravis and has acquired the name because the nematode was first discovered in soil beside the river Americans call the Rio Grande and Mexicans name the Rio Bravo. The discovery of riobravis is a fascinating detective story but peripheral to our play. The scientists at the Agricultural Research Service lab. in Texas found riobravis, observed its behavior and established methods for its reproduction in huge numbers. This information was given to several commercial companies that now produce and market it.

There are "good" nematodes and "bad" nematodes in the eyes of man, and riobravis is beneficial to man because it is very destructive to "bad" insects, not harmful to "good" insects and has no known deleterious environmental effects—riobravis is a good guy. The scientists that discovered it are so enthusiastic that some of their literature bears the title *Riobravis: Nematode the Magnificent.* I mentioned that it is tiny and the suppliers deal in units of billions of riobravis. From the numbers I have seen, 1 billion riobravis would weigh about 0.75 lb. Or your average riobravis would come in at about 0.00000000075 lb. Pretty small.

A maintenance crew with George in the lead enters stage right and in the proper time and manner fling riobravis in an amount of 1 billion of the tiny guys per acre. The stage lights dim as each riobravis descends into the soil in search of the evil cricket. Like a good bloodhound, the nematode follows a scent trail to it prey, and once the cricket is encountered its doom is sealed. Riobravis traverses its body like a Lilliputian challenged by the enormity of slumbering Gulliver until it finds entrance through a pore or other opening.

And now the plot thickens. Riobravis does not enter the huge cricket alone and unarmed. No, it carries in its own tiny body a specific strain of bacteria, and we won't bother to calculate their weight. The bacteria reproduce continually and as they pass out of riobravis and into the body of the cricket they cause a septicemia that kills the bad cricket within 48 hours. Nematode offspring feed on the corpse and produce a second generation termed infective juveniles. These nematodes in the body of the cricket, one-fortieth of an inch long and numbering 300,000 or more, leave to search nearby soil for new prey. Once mole crickets are eliminated, riobravis will disappear through natural mortality.

CURTAIN!

As the curtain slowly descends on this *Happy Ending*, it is marvelous to contemplate that the concatenation of events just related take place so that the two species, golfer and gull alike and each in its own fashion, may enjoy the carefully groomed turf of the Ocean Golf Course, free of poisonous chemicals.

Welcoming Committee Alert: Another New Family May Join Us Soon

The name on the mailbox will read *Canis latrans*. The family is well established and famous in song and legend in the Far West, where their neighbors just call them coyotes. The sheepherders and cattle ranchers have never liked their lifestyle and slaughtered them in the countless thousands. Nevertheless, the family has managed not only to survive but also to increase in numbers. More recently, they have begun to expand their territory eastward. Splendidly adapted to the open, brushy western territory, coyotes previously had little reason to enter heavily forested eastern areas. However, by the time survivors of the carnage began dispersing, people had cleared much of those forests; thereby, creating a splendid habitat for them. The family accepted the invitation, and soon state game agencies were reporting coyotes in residence and multiplying in numbers all through the eastern half of the country.

Once established, the family expands rapidly and the population can quadruple in a single year, because each female is astoundingly reproductive. She is capable of bearing as many as *19* in a litter! In our state of South Carolina, coyotes were first reported along the Savannah River as early as 1979. Therefore, it was no surprise when coyotes were sighted in Charleston County in the late 1980s, and now they are so plentiful in Colleton County that they are listed in that county's commercial harvest records for trappers. (Twenty-four were trapped there last year.) Because they are excellent swimmers, they are unlikely to neglect Kiawah Island, for we have much to offer. Everything from our abundant voles to young fawns are welcome items on their dinner plate; also, they have a high tolerance for humans and feel quite at home in a habitat of woods interspersed with open spaces, a common pattern on Kiawah.

So, they may be on our doorstep even now, and we should know something about our new neighbors. Because we are not in the business of raising livestock, it is to be hoped the relationship will be better than in the west. The coyote is one of the most primitive of the canid, and it has a just claim to existence here for its ancestors arrived on this continent several million years ago. Its menu is both long and varied. It will happily accept berries as an appetizer and it is not above scarfing up grasshoppers and other insects as it goes along. Mainly however, it depends upon a wide selection of animals and birds for its meat course. It is able and willing to ambush, trail, run down, pounce upon, sniff out, dig up and overpower all kinds of rodents—as we stand to applaud on the sidelines. Its menu also includes snakes, frogs, opossums, otters, raccoons, but hopefully not our cats and small dogs. As mentioned, even deer are not beyond their capability, and these usually are fawns and debilitated adults.

Coyotes live in packs and stay in touch by yipping more frequently than the classic howl that appears in all the western literature. The family is cohesive and pairing usually is for life. After breeding in February or March, the pair will dig a den or borrow one, sometimes from a fox. There, the female will give birth about 63 days later to all those pups. The male faithfully will deliver food for about 2 months to his mate as she nurses the squealing, squirming, whining, young family.

When the coyote arrives on Kiawah, the ecological balance will need to be readjusted between all the other carnivores that now live here. There will be competition for a limited amount of prey, and in some cases a predator may find the new animal viewing it as the prey. It should be quite interesting to follow these changes. For those of you that watch for wildlife on the island, the coyote has the general appearance of a small German shepherd dog. You may easily dismiss it as a dog on the loose, but who will be the first to claim a sighting? No fair mistaking our famous cougar for the first coyote!

The Restless Nature of Beach Sand

The beach is a delightful panorama; we are overwhelmed with the immensity of space, but we are more intrigued with the small changes that continually occur. It is this sense of stirring and transition that draw us there again and again. Clouds pass serenely above the rolling waves as sandpipers play tag with the wave fronts, while crabs scurry by on import errands, and even the sand beneath our feet responds to wind and wave. This movement of sand is the most difficult to perceive because it occurs so gradually, but it ultimately determines the character of the beach. The contour of the beach is changed by the coastal current, and the current in turn changes with the periodic accumulation of sand shoals in the delta of the Stono Inlet. The current that normally runs from east to west and parallel to the beach may be deflected landward when a shoal builds up, and erosion may occur near the center of the beach. After the shoal migrates and attaches along the easternmost mile of Kiawah's shoreline, sand is distributed all along the beach. Then, the erosion usually is corrected over a period of several years.

A new shoal has accumulated at the Stono Inlet over the past few years, and now we are seeing the resulting erosion at the midsection of the beach, particularly in the area of Windswept Villas. But be patient, other changes are occurring, and the central portion of the beach should be restored in the future. The shoal has become attached to the end of Kiawah and its sand has begun to be redistributed along the beach. The Kiawah Island Town Council in March of 1996 decided, for aesthetic reasons, to hasten the natural process by renourishment of the dunes where erosion has been most severe. Two creaking, old, rusty bulldozers crept out and laboriously scraped approximately 30,000 cubic yards of sand from the lower beach and deposited it at the escarpment of the upper beach.

The Town Council needed to be reassured that no deleterious effects had occurred during the alteration. Therefore, they requested that the Marine Resources Division of the South Carolina Dept. of Natural Resources analyze core samples from scraped and unaltered sections of the beach. These comparisons revealed that the scraping had not altered the physical composition of the beach which consists of about 93% fine sand, 5% finely pulverized shells and 1% or less of each of silt, clay and organic matter. Therefore, it was concluded that the sand relocation had not significantly altered the beach, either in its physical properties or its suitability as a habitat for the fauna that dwell in the sand.

These analytical results were not unexpected, because the beaches all along the South Carolina coast are quite uniform in composition. The reason is that they are all sustained from a huge offshore reservoir of sand on the continental shelf. The ancient deposits of sand that rest there were brought down from the Appalachian Mountains many millions of years ago by the streams and rivers. At that time the mountains were snow-capped giants, guarding the American coast as this continent was forced away from Europe and Africa by an expanding Atlantic Ocean.

Now, the sand from the disintegration of the mountains is spread thinly over the entire continental shelf. Often the layer of sand is less than ten feet deep, so that outcrops of bedrock and old coral reefs commonly are revealed to the scuba divers as they cruise over those benthic plains. But how does the sand get up to our beach without the clanking bulldozers that we rely upon? Even at the edge of the continental shelf, at depths of 300 feet and more, wave action is forever nudging grains of sand up toward the land. In all this slow but inexorable process, there is a gentle winnowing and sieving in which the smaller grains are separated from the larger and so are selectively brought toward our beaches. So the next time you walk the beach, recall that you walk upon sand older than the landmarks customarily associated with timelessness such as the Rocky Mountains or the Grand Canyon of the west.

Once the sand grain is in the surf, its travels are not over. As it surges back and forth in response to the ebb and flow of each arriving wave, it is carried down beach in a western direction by the longshore current. People that like to play with the numbers of waves/minute and the speed of the current calculate that a grain of sand on our beach will move westward about five miles or half the total distance of our beach in a year's time. Therefore, it is not surprising that the sand spit at Captain Sam's Inlet builds up rapidly.

Even when the sand grain is carried by high tides to a distance well above normal wave action, its travels are not over. There the wind participates as it whiskbrooms the beach and remodels the dunes. You can sense the winnowing action of the wind if you lightly drag your feet over the dry sand of the upper beach. The loosely packed tiny grains emit a soft squeaking sound as they slide by one another beneath your feet. They are still in the process of moving elsewhere.

A Young Cardinal's First Bath

All through June, my bird feeder, tucked beneath the branches of a fan palm, is surrounded by a flurry of juvenile cardinals with their characteristic subdued plumage and black beaks. They cluster around their harried dad, and if he is overwhelmed with his duties, they push past and learn for themselves the basics of selecting and shelling a sunflower seed. Nearby is a bath that also gets a lot of attention from the birds One of the young cardinals must have seen other birds enjoying the bath, for it alighted on the rim. It stared down intently as though trying to determine the depth, first with head cocked on one side and then on the other. Gaining courage, it hopped in and stood rigidly still. Slowly its feathers fluffed up, but it remained motionless. Then, it began tentatively to dip first one wing and then the other. Soon it was flapping vigorously and water was cascading out as though it were the centerpiece of an elaborate fountain. After several minutes, it finally hopped back on the rim in quite a bedraggled state. Flapping and shaking vigorously once again, it put itself back in order and then gave a long stretch as though to say, "Wow, this life isn't half bad!" Then off it went to rejoin its family at the feeder.

Summer, 1997

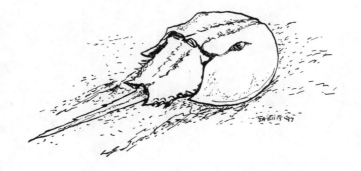

The
Horseshoe
Crab

Most beach walkers have a
nodding acquaintance with
this strange beast, but to
describe it for the uninitiated is a challenge. Perhaps by resort-
ing to bits and pieces of other animate and inanimate objects, I
can create a descriptive assembly. If you are fortunate enough to
see it in action, the creature looks like a little armored tank as it
lurches up the beach. Seeing it lying quietly in the beach sand,
you might think it a fossil protruding from some prehistoric
seabed. This is true in an evolutionary sense, for its ancestors
were among the first animals to come out of the sea. Its fossils
go back without significant change for over 200 million years.

Its body is covered with a stiff carapace of chitin, much like
the material of a human fingernail. As its name implies, the shell
had the shape of a horseshoe except that it is far too large for the
hoof of even the giant Percheron. Adding further menace is a
rapier like appendage where a tail should be, or is that thing
some sort of stinger? No, it is a stiff spike, termed a telson, that
serves as a levering device. When the animal swims shoreward,
the surf may fling it on its back; using the telson it can flip over
and plod onward.

If you gain the courage to tip it over, and if it is still alive, your examination will probably come to a hasty end as bizarre body parts of menacing mien wave about, although it is really harmless. If it is dead, you may gain the courage to count six pairs of legs like tractor treads that fill the center of the body cavity. The mouth is located between the rows of legs, and posterior to the legs is another structure that reflects its antediluvian lineage. Here the large book gills are packed together like leaves of an ancient manuscript.

This strange creature belongs to the phylum Arthropoda, those animals with jointed legs and a chitinous exoskeleton. This huge phylum includes everything from insects to crustaceans, and the horseshoe crab occupies a separate subclass. Indeed, it is very exclusive for its only living relatives are two related species found in the mangrove swamps of Southeast Asia. Actually it is not a crab at all but a descendant from the ancient line of Merostomates, marine arachnids, and to our amazement, its closest living relatives are the spiders and scorpions.

The Atlantic horseshoe crab that we encounter on the beach occurs all along the coast from Bar Harbor, Maine to the Gulf of Mexico. As water temperature drops in the fall, it moves into deeper water and burrows into bottom sediments. Then early in the spring, although buried in ocean sediments many fathoms beneath the surface, it somehow senses the moment for the annual migration. An internal chronometer set by the changing hours of daylight may tip it off, or it may respond to a rise in water temperature. Struggling out of the sediment, it has the ability to swim awkwardly in an upside down position, but it will spend most of the time crawling through bottom sand and muck in search of the molluscs and worms that are its main food.

Later in the spring, they will crawl landward and beach themselves for mating, as they have been doing generation after generation for millions of years. Sexual reproduction is always beset with difficulties, as we all know, but for both partners to be encased in armor adds enormously to the problem. However, over time the horseshoe crab has worked it out quite nicely. The much larger female, within an hour of high tide, crawls up the beach and digs into the sand just below the high tide mark. There she deposits eggs in shallow scraped hollows in the sand. During this time, several of the smaller males have been pursuing her, and now they attach themselves in sequence behind her. Dragging them along, each firmly attached to her or to the next in line by specially modified front legs that serve as claspers, she drags them over her deposited eggs. Fertilization of the eggs occurs in boisterous congo-line fashion to the rhythm of the rippling surf and the chorus of excited gulls overhead.

Each female lays thousands of the clear greenish eggs, about one-eighth of an inch in diameter, in each of several nests. These are a tremendous bonanza for migratory shorebirds, and they feed upon them avidly for their high content of fats and proteins. The embryonic crabs that survive this onslaught have only two weeks to develop in the eggs before the sun, earth and new moon line up to produce the next spring tide. Then, the hatchlings fight the pull of gravity and push up through the sand to ride the receding waters into the ocean. The young, just the color of the sand, are perfect miniatures of the adults. They remain inshore for a time, and occasionally the beachcomber is fortunate enough to find a cluster of them on the beach, each about one-half an inch in diameter.

Like the true crab, the horseshoe crab also casts its hard shell and grows a larger one as it develops. If you are inclined to collect the shell of this critter to hang on the wall, be sure you select a cast shell and not one loaded with odoriferous body parts. You can distinguish the empty shell by the fracture line around the front rim, at the top of the shell, where the softbodied animal exited. Then you may safely hang it on your wall as a reminder that some animals seem to ignore Darwin's theory of evolution.

Oystercatcher

I happened upon my first oyster-catcher nest while patrolling the perimeter of a noisy Least tern colony at the eastern end of Kiawah. Both Wilson's plovers and American oystercatchers often place their nests near tern colonies; they seem to depend upon the aggressive terns to repel the predators. In the bland similarity of shorebirds, the oyster-catcher stands out by virtue of its large size, dramatic appearance and regal bearing. It is dressed in formal black and white attire, accentuated with a huge red bill and an almost demonic pair of bright yellow eyes rimmed with crimson.

In summer, oystercatchers are solitary and fiercely territorial. Prior to finding the nest by the tern colony, I had observed two males engaged in the rivalry of courtship for a female. All three paced meticulously back and forth, like robed judges on a difficult case, with pauses to bow courteously to one another; suddenly, the mood would change with wild calls coming from beaks thrown skyward. Then, the solemn pacing would resume. At some juncture beyond my perception and by a mysterious alchemy that I do not comprehend, a bonding occurred. The female joined with her chosen mate to drive away the rejected suitor. So, I was not too surprised to come upon the nest two weeks later. Tracks of the mated pair lead me to it, situated upon a sand hummock with a good view all around. The nest was just a scraped out depression in the center of the hummock, and within it were two eggs, nearly the size of hen's eggs, of an olive-buff color plus some speckling of darker brown.

Not wanting to disturb the oystercatchers more than necessary, I used a spotting scope on subsequent days to observe the nest from a distance of 300-400 yards. Incubation was long and conditions that summer were severe on that open strip of sand. On extremely hot days, I could see the bird panting from the heat as she stood above the eggs to shade them and permit as much cooling as possible from any passing breeze. (Others who might wish to observe these nesting shorebirds should take note and not keep the parent from the nest.) Still other harsh conditions prevailed, and once strong winds from the southwest buried nests of the Least terns beneath drifting sand. Through it all, the oystercatcher sat stoically on her own nest.

After three weeks, the eggs hatched, and all shell fragments were promptly removed by one of the parents who flew off with the pieces to drop them well away from the nest. The two chicks, matching the color of the sand, were so well camouflaged that I had difficulty seeing them even though I knew the nest location. At my approach, they were flattened down together so that they resembled a small, inconspicuous hummock of sand rather than two live chicks.

By the next day, the chicks had left the nest, and were scurrying about beneath the cover of low vegetation in the dunes. Alarmed at my approach, one of the parents gave a low whistled warning; the two chicks crouched motionless, and blended completely into the sand.

The feeding techniques used by oystercatchers are difficult to learn and require long practice. During all that time, the parents continue to feed the juveniles, giving them bits of oyster and other shellfish. I had the opportunity to observe one lesson as it was given on the beach later in the summer. The two parents and the two juveniles worked in pairs, one adult with one juvenile. The parent would search for whelks just beneath surface at the surf line. When a whelk was located, the bird would use its beak to burrow beneath the tip of the shell and lift it enough to be able to deftly reach in and grasp a fleshy portion of the whelk. The juvenile watched intently, and then stepped forward to take the morsel. Once during the lesson, the occupant of the shell was a hermit crab, and the young bird was having a difficult time with the pugnacious crab until the parent stepped up and killed it.

The oystercatchers feed on oysters also, as their name implies, but they do this on the back side of the island where the oyster beds are located in the marsh creek beds. At that time "oystereater" might be a better name for these birds since the stationary oysters require little "catching." However, ingenuity is required again to attack the mollusc within its armor of shell. There are two schools of thought amongst the oystercatchers on this matter of opening an oyster. Some of the birds sneak up on the unsuspecting bivalve with its shells partially opened for circulation of water during feeding. The bird quickly stabs its blade-like beak between the valves and cuts the adductor muscle that closes the shells. This has been termed the "stabber" approach. Others make a more direct, brutal attack. They hammer the shell with a series of well-directed short blows until a hole is formed and the bill can be thrust in to sever the adductor muscle. Not too surprisingly, this has been termed the "hammerer" approach.

Both of these approaches are learned techniques and an individual bird will employ just one or the other technique, depending upon how it was taught. Biologists have demonstrated this by exchanging eggs between nests of "hammers" and "stabbers," and later observing the feeding behavior of the chicks. It was concluded that the behavior is learned from the foster parent, not genetically transmitted from the true parent. Thus, a chick reared by "hammerers" becomes a "hammerer," although it came from an egg laid by a "stabber," and vice versa. I have not had the opportunity to ask these biologists what happens when a "hammerer" and a "stabber" pair up to raise a family. But perhaps this is all worked out during courtship.

Observation of tagged birds has shown that these feeding skills take a long time to perfect. Birds after one year were still clumsy and inefficient. Even three-year olds had not attained the weight of breeding adults, and it is customary for oyster-catchers not to mate before their fourth year. Until then, they simply could not cope with the demands of raising a brood. However, the passing on to the young of feeding skills is probably of great advantage to the species. If an oystercatcher discovers a new source of food, or develops a new technique, it can pass that knowledge on to its young and ultimately to the whole population

After the strict seclusion of each nesting pair during the summer, the oystercatchers in winter become quite sociable. They gather in flocks, and one large flock has spent the winter along the Kiawah River for many years. The majority of the birds in the flock are undoubtedly migrants from the north that join our resident birds for the winter. They can often be seen loafing close together on the mud flats. At other times, you may see the flock flying low over the river with strong, swift strokes, and displaying the large red beak leading the flashing black and white wing pattern at each stroke.

Macrofauna: The Little Animals That Dwell in the Intertidal Zone of the Beach

Earlier this spring, in a story entitled The Restless Nature of Beach Sand; I described a beach renourishment that had been undertaken by the Kiawah Island Town Council in the spring of 1996. Approximately 30,000 cubic yards of sand were scraped from the intertidal zone between the low water level and the high tide line. To the casual beach stroller, this appears to be a desolate zone occupied by an occasional shorebird or a few tiny fish trapped in a tidal slough. Therefore, any disturbance of this intertidal zone would not seem to have any significant effect on the ecology of the beach.

Certainly, this zone would appear like a ghetto for marine life. Enemies with huge mouths abound in the surf, making survival a constant challenge. Unending waves sweep up and rip currents push and tug. The temperature and salinity rise and fall like the waves. Life at the tide-line is literally a roller coaster ride, and when an organism finally gets its feet on the ground, sea and sand slip from beneath it.

And yet, the zone is teaming with life. Tiny invertebrates ranging in size from those retained by a 0.5-mm sieve up to three-quarters of an inch in length live in the top four to six inches of the sediment. In one square yard of this zone, marine biologists often find more than 35,000 of these animals. Dr. Robert Van Dolah, director of the SC Marine Resources Division (SCMRD), has told me that more than eighty different kinds of organisms have been collected from the intertidal zone on the beaches of South Carolina.

This is largely a community of crustaceans, molluscs and worms that are collectively termed macrofauna, although they may seem micro to us. They constitute an important link in the food chain, for they consume the truly microflora and microfauna, the plankton brought in by the sea, as well as the detritus that accumulates in this zone. The foods thus fixed at this first level are then passed on as essential foodstuffs for the larger invertebrates, nearshore fish and wading shorebirds.

The concern of the town council was that this community might be destroyed as sand was moved to the upper beach. Tests on other beaches in the area have been reassuring in this regard, for they have shown that beach scraping is normally followed by a rapid recovery of the invertebrate fauna without significant changes in diversity. To ensure that a similar recovery pattern had occurred on the Kiawah beach, the town council contracted with the SCMRD to conduct a survey approximately 60 days after the scraping. Core samples were taken in the intertidal zone both at locations that had been scraped and others that were undisturbed. All biological samples were processed at the SCMRD laboratory at Ft. Johnson under the supervision of Dr. Van Dolah and Martin Levisen. After sieving to remove sand, the macrofauna were stained with a Rose Bengal stain to enhance their visibility and then identified taxonomically under a microscope.

The 20 composite core samples collected from both study areas contained 26 different species of macrofauna. The numerically dominant species were the coquina clam (*Donax vaiabilis*) and four species of amphipods that resemble miniature shrimp, which is natural because the two are closely related taxonomically. These totaled 89.7% of all the organisms that were found. One species of the polychaete worm was the only other species that contributed greater than 2% to the overall community structure. In the conclusion of the report, it was stated that the data "did not indicate any long-term adverse impacts to the beach infaunal communities." In fact, recovery appeared to have occurred quite rapidly in view of the fact that sampling was done only sixty days after the scraping.

The two major inhabitants of the community, the coquina clam and the digger amphipod (or one of its close relatives) may be easily observed by the curious beach explorer, for both of these are within the upper size range of 1/4–3/4 inches. Equipped with your fine-mesh kitchen strainer or a goldfish net, scoop up a sample of sand from the intertidal zone. Lower the container sufficiently into the water to permit the sand to be washed out, and you are likely to retain your specimen. "My hand lens, please."

The shrimp-like amphipods are excellent burrowers with legs especially modified for this purpose, and often they are among the first animals to colonize a scraped or renourished beach. They take advantage of the fluid condition of the sand in the swash zone for lateral movement across considerable distances, leading to rapid recolonization of the scraped zones.

The coquina clam with its wedge-shaped shell is known for its subtle variations in pastel colors that range from pure white to yellow, rose, lavender, pale blue and deep purple, interspersed with darker rays of color. If they were larger, they would adorn the mantelpiece of every beachcomber on the island. These clams are far from sedentary, for their survival in that turbulent beach zone depends upon their speed of digging down through the fluid sand. With each wash of surf, they are exposed, and when the wave recedes each one rapidly thrusts its hatchet-shaped foot down through the sand, expands the tip into an anchor and pulls itself downward. Within two or three such thrusts, it can pull itself beneath the surface. Then up go the siphon tubes and filter feeding is back in operation. They are no slouches even though they are clams! They do this in unison with all their neighbors after each wave, so the collector will see hundreds of the colorful little clams all lurching down into the shifting sands like puppets on strings at the close of a marionette show.

Do your collecting in the warm weather, however, for in winter they burrow deeper beneath the sand or perish from the cold. Then you will find windrows of their empty shells numbering in the many thousands washed up along the wrack line.

Are Some of Our Juvenile Osprey Lacking in Parental Guidance?

I have often seen osprey parents bring twigs and Spanish moss to the nest during the time chicks were present. I had always assumed it was just good housekeeping for the maintenance of the nest. Always, the chicks showed great interest in the way the new materials were worked into the nest, and now I suspect the parents had a second reason for this performance. This must be their only opportunity to teach the chicks this essential skill of nest construction.

I was prompted to draw this conclusion when I observed the pair of ospreys that I termed the "newly-weds" who failed nesting last year. (See page 77.) This year, judging by their performance, the same pair was back at the same excellent nesting site. They worked sporadically at the nest all spring but never could get it to a size that would hold an egg. As last seen, one of the two brought a nice clump of moss, but did not place it in the nest and trod it down as is the standard procedure. Tentatively, it pulled some strands from the clump and got its foot caught in the remainder. Finally, it dropped the strands, untangled its foot and flew off. Must the Bluebird nestbox team now take on a new assignment, building nests for ospreys with delinquent parents?

Fall, 1997

Animal Tracks Challenge Our Detective Skills

We know very little about the activities of most of the mammals on Kiawah, because they are nocturnal and concealed from our sight. Therefore, we must depend upon their tracks to tell us where they roamed and what they did during the night. In the interior of the island, this is difficult to do, because leaves and pine needles often cover the tracks. One way of overcoming this difficulty is to attract animals to a cleared and smoothed site. The trick is to attract animals to the prepared area, and scent is customarily used as the attractant. Not too surprising, such a plot is called a scent station. The cleared area, about one square yard, is lightly dusted with powdered lime to enhance the pattern of tracks, and a small disc of a volatile, odoriferous compound highly attractive to most carnivorous animals is placed in the center of the plot.

The next morning, tracks of the nocturnal visitors should be clear for identification. Marks from the cloven hooves of the deer are the easiest to identify, but the nearly human handprints of the raccoon are quickly learned too. The round paw prints of the fox and bobcat are more difficult, and inspection of claw

NATURE'S WAY ON KIAWAH

marks becomes critical for the discerning sleuth. Beyond that, tracks of birds, snakes, alligators and possibly even the legendary cougar add their challenges.

But the very best tracks and the tales that they tell are to be found on the beach. The damp sand will faithfully record the passing of everything from the heavy tread of the deer to the light prints of the mice that dwell in the dunes and wander in search of seeds and grasses.

The long slanting light of early morning is ideal for revealing tracks. Take your gaze away from the magical interplay of sunlight on the clouds, for ahead of you is a great sweep of beach sand, a freshly printed book, waiting to be read for the first time. Animal prints show up best during that magical hour following sunrise when their outlines are crisp and clear. By breakfast time on a hot summer's day, the sun has dried the sand so that it begins to crumble and blur the prints. A wind may have sprung up and sand may have drifted over them, or a rising tide could erase them completely.

Animal tracks extend the time frame, they tell us not only who came by earlier but often by studying the tracks, they tell us something about what the critter was doing. It can be a challenging game, and there is no better place to start than the beach. I remember coming across a furrow in the sand that led up beach to the carcass of a dead cormorant. All signs indicated that it had been dragged up from lower on the beach. What animal had done that? Observation of the opening of a Ghost crab burrow alongside the carcass gave the first clue. Did the crab happen upon the carcass at that spot and dig a new residence beside it? No, further inspection showed the tracks of the crab alongside the furrow made by the carcass. The crab had been the one that dragged the carcass about six feet up the beach to its home burrow. This was an example of the incredible strength of such an animal. The weight of the cormorant must have been twenty or thirty fold greater than that of the Ghost crab, and the feat is reminiscent of the huge loads that ants can carry back to their nest. Both of these arthropods, with their rigid exoskeletons, are built on an entirely different body plan from we soft-bodied mammals.

The turtle patrol engages in this sort of detective work all through the summer. The nesting patrol members depend entirely upon the track of the female turtle to inform them of the presence of a nest. By analyzing the pattern of the track, they can select the in-bound track that the turtle made in crawling up the beach, and follow the track to the nesting site. Most volunteers soon acquire the additional skill of reading the nesting site in order to probe correctly for the nest.

If the nest had been raided prior to the arrival of the patrol, the tracks of the culprit permits identification. The patrol may find the tracks of a fox following up the larger track of the nesting turtle. So, the animals play the same detective game. And sometimes the fox prints reveal the presence of one or more young kits following their mother and learning the basics for procuring a breakfast of turtle eggs.

At hatching time, the patrols must sort out the tiny tracks of the hatchlings as they make their way to the ocean and distinguish them from tracks of their predators, the Ghost crabs. When the two sets of tracks intersect, we know a small tragedy has occurred. If the track ends at the mouth of a crab burrow, we know that one more hatchling must be crossed off our list of survivors.

Now, return to the beach in the morning with an alert eye and a questing mind. Good sleuthing!

The Developer Is
Creating Ecotones
on Kiawah

Before you conclude from the title that an ecotone is a serious blemish or even contagious and begin mentally to compose your Letter to the Editor, let me explain. Biologists employ the term "ecotone" to refer to any border between two habitats such as the edge between a woods and a fairway, pond or marsh, or even a roadway.

The edge of the sea, where the continent and the ocean join, is the greatest of all ecotones. We have considered in the story, Macrofauna: The Little Animals that Dwell in the Intertidal Zone of the Beach, the immense diversity of invertebrate organisms that occupy that zone on the beach. These intertidal zones supply marine food chains with nutrients, serve as nurseries for an array of ocean fauna and play essential roles in the life cycles of many fish and shellfish.

In the interior of Kiawah Island, the developer has been busy creating new edges or ecotones. Is that good or bad as far as wildlife is concerned? The answer depends upon the species, because various ecotones favor some animals and birds over others. Some birds such as flycatchers, vireos and many of the warblers require woodlands and these will diminish with the development of the island. Others such as the mockingbird, many of the sparrows, wrens, mourning dove, and catbird thrive on edges and open spaces. Thoughts of the nefarious cowbird who lays her eggs in the nests of other birds will spring in the minds of many, and it is true that the cowbird is one of the species favored by open spaces.

As a digression, something might be said in defense of the cowbird. She has had her problems too. Flocks of cowbirds, as the name implies, traditionally followed the roaming herds of buffalo. Like the Cattle egrets, they fed upon the insects stirred out of concealment by the hooves of the grazing animals. The cowbird didn't have the time to sit around on eggs while her herd disappeared over the hill. Hence, she did the next best thing; she dumped her eggs in the nests of other more settled species for incubation and rearing.

In the overall assessment, ecotones increase both the number and diversity of species. Every birder soon learns that the way to see a large variety of birds in a short time is to plan field trips that include various ecotones. The reason is that birds commonly require more things for survival than can be had from a single habitat such as a dense woods or an open field. If their needs can be met by using both habitats, their chances for survival are increased. And that's where they'll be, at the border. The field may provide insects or seeds for food and grass for lining nests; the woods may have twigs for the nest and protective cover from enemies. The chief reason for high population densities of birds in parks and gardens is the rich interspersion of trees, shrubs, lawns, walks, flowerbeds, pools and even buildings.

The Kiawah Island Naturalists' Club has had first-hand experience with ecotones on many field trips; also, we viewed them from another aspect during a field trip one October to Mingo Point. Twenty-five different species of shrubs, trees and vines were loaded with seeds, fruits and other foodstuffs along the border between the dense thickets and the open areas. This availability of natural foods is why your feeders are deserted in the fall, but the hungry birds will return once these supplies are consumed.

We noted on the field trip that deer, foxes, raccoons and opossums also eat many of these foods. In fact, these animals just named are termed "edge" species because they occur most frequently at edges or borders between different types of habitat. They use these ecotones as corridors as they move about to secure food and water. The term "greenways" is the buzzword in vogue these days for these corridors, and greenways are plentiful on Kiawah. To ensure that these corridors remain in the future, it will be important to retain generous setbacks behind homes on golf course fairways, marsh perimeters and pond edges. Preservation of these greenways is another contribution that both the developer and the property owner can make to the welfare of wildlife on the island.

On Kiawah, we have "brownways" in addition to greenways. I refer to the immense corridor of dunes that many of the birds, mammals and reptiles use for various purposes. Some use them primarily as corridors on their travels about the island; others such as the deer use the myrtle and holly thickets as shelter during the daytime; still others make the dunes their permanent home. Let's never overlook this important function of the huge area that is so essential for the continued well being of much of our wildlife.

Rookery Pond

The herons and egrets are a gregarious bunch that prefer to nest together in noisy, crowded colonies called rookeries. They are like their human counterparts who also nest together, and demand good home sites, police protection and availability of good shopping centers. So too, these birds are very selective in their choice of a rookery. There must sufficient tree canopy to accommodate all the nests spaced just one beak-peck apart, there must be protection from the many predators eager to devour their precious eggs and chicks and there must be a plentiful supply of nutritious food close by to feed those ravenous youngsters. Within recent times, only one swampy pond on Kiawah seemed to meet all these requirements. It is now just pond #32 in the community association records, the pond that runs alongside Turtle Beach Lane in the middle of the island.

As shown in a chart of Kiawah dated 1854 and reproduced in the *Environmental Inventory of Kiawah Island*, the land surrounding the little pond was under cultivation in the 19th century, but the wetland itself was probably left undisturbed. The same historical source, in its 1974–75 survey of birds on Kiawah stated that the small pond, then called The Rookery, was the only site on Kiawah for breeding by wading birds. The rookery was confined to a dense stand of low swamp willows that grew in the midst of the tiny wetland. Seven species were reported to be breeding there at that time. Cattle egrets were the most numerous with 50 nests, other species were the Anhinga, Common egret, Snowy egret, Green heron, Louisiana heron and Little Blue heron for a total of 145 nests.

According to my Field Notes, I first discovered or rather rediscovered The Rookery one morning early in May of 1979. This was before construction of the Turtle Point Golf Course was begun later in the same year. I can remember as though it were yesterday hearing a noisy commotion of birds ahead of me as I wandered through the woods on that morning. Leaving the shady shelter of the trees, I entered a sunny field that is now the 17th hole of the golf course. Pushing my way through the dense brush and over tangles of brambles and vines, I came upon the wetland completely overgrown with tall cattails—and there in the center were the swamp willows. The low trees stood together in a tight green cluster with branches drooping in typical willow fashion, intertwining and reaching down to touch the surface of the shallow pool in which they grew. Overhead, herons and egrets were flying in and out of the swamp in large numbers, calling all the while.

As I pressed further into the swamp for a closer look, I could see through the dense tangle of the willows two large alligators floating side by side in the water. I counted 27 flimsy nests of slender sticks precariously balanced on the branches above the patient alligators. Transfixed, I continued to watch the bustling scene as herons and egrets continually arrived and departed with flailing wings and loud cries that announced their arrivals and departures in a medley of dialects. Common and Snowy egrets as well as Green herons were well represented, while three Anhingas soared overhead. However, it was not the best of places for an inexperienced naturalist to visit, and I unwisely lingered too long. As I staggered out, I found I was now bearing a heavy load of ticks, and later found to my distress that chiggers also had taken advantage of my innocence.

A tight little set of ecological relationships made this rookery possible. The cattails and water-loving swamp willows had filled the wetland. The wading birds were attracted to the secluded site by the plentiful fish, snakes and frogs; they stayed to nest because the low willows provided a secure nesting site. The site was secure because the water beneath the trees dissuaded the usual nest predators such as bobcats, raccoons, and snakes, and the alligators ensured that they would keep their distance. In compensation, the alligators consumed the chicks that fell from the nests, but then, those unfortunate chicks were doomed in any event. So, this delicate balance of wildlife and habitat had remained intact for decades and possibly centuries.

Following construction of the golf course, the luxuriant plant-life of the wetland remained undisturbed. Birds continued to forage there for food, but they no longer found it suitable for nesting. The next major change was wrought by Hurricane Hugo in 1989, as it yanked up most of the weakly rooted willows. Thereafter, the developer made the decision to convert the swamp into a lagoon; all vegetation was removed and the pond was dredged to its present depth. Now, it is one more attractive lagoon on the island, but the herons and egrets must travel elsewhere to rear their chicks.

Kiawah Swamp Garden: A Microhabitat in Transition

Kiawah Swamp Garden, located at the end of Turtle Beach Lane, is a tiny remnant of a freshwater wetland. The little pond was dumped upon, neglected and vilified while all the surrounding land underwent profound changes into golf course fairway and beachfront home sites. It managed to maintain its integrity and its continued isolation because of the presence of a dike that separates it from the pond that was described earlier as The Rookery. The dike that separated the two ponds in earlier times had constituted a portion of the boundary line between Shoolbred property to the west and Vanderhorst property to the east. It served as a safe pathway to the beach through the extensive wetland that formerly ran all along the present chain of lagoons. To the east is The Rookery, to the west is a small, nameless lagoon, and beyond it lies the last of the unaltered wetland.

The perplexing question was what to do with the tiny residual patch now known as the Swamp Garden. Some of us felt that it should be preserved in a natural state as a microhabitat representative of the original freshwater swamps that had existed on the island prior to development. A path of bark mulch was placed upon the ancient dike and extended through the lowland around the pond. For completion, a little wooden bridge spanned the wetter portion of the little garden.

Natural vegetation was encouraged and supplemented with other plants characteristic of such a freshwater wetland. As the character of the natural habitat began to return, the native animal and bird life came back of their own accord. These included the Boat-tailed grackles and Red-winged blackbirds that sing and nest in the reeds, the alligators, turtles and snakes that sun on the half submerged trees, and the wading birds—the herons and egrets—that enjoy the plentiful food in that secluded setting.

Mother Nature once again took an interest. She decreed that a sun-lit, shallow, freshwater pond protected from the wind by an encirclement of bushes and trees should have a healthy growth of Duckweed on the surface. To some of those living in the neighborhood, this seemed to be going too far in a back-to-nature movement. The Duckweed appeared to them as green scum and vigorous protests were made to poor Norm Shea, the lagoon manager, who was only trying to put the habitat back together. Examined closely, Duckweed is a very attractive tiny floating aquatic plant that looks like a miniature edition of a pond lily. There are several species but typically, it consists of one or more oval fronds of a glistening dark green color perhaps 1/8 of an inch or less in diameter and with a single white root extending down below each frond.

At first Norm and his assistant, Janet Ellis, heeded the complaints and tried to argue with Mother Nature. They skimmed off Duckweed by the hour, but it was like trying to dry out the beach with a pail and sponge. Now, they are hoping that the introduction of Mosquito fish for mosquito control and Tillapia fish for consumption of the Duckweed and other undesirable aquatic vegetation will provide more open water. Then, the garden may become acceptable both to Mother Nature and to those who think we really need a more civilized Swamp Garden in the middle of the island.

Today, a good compromise seems possible. The entrance is defined by a bulletin board informative about the purpose of the garden and items of seasonal interest, the trail is clear and well surfaced with mulch, many of the interesting plants are identified with small placards, and the small animals and birds are usually out on display. Come visit it!

Epilogue

*T*hus, we end this chapter in ongoing events on Kiawah.
Walk your own trails.
Make your own observations.
Build your own stories.
Of Nature's Way on this wonderful planet,
Sheathed in pulsating, warm and vibrant life!